The Sew-Easy
Guide To Menswear

The Sew-Easy Guide To Menswear

or How to Keep Him in Stitches

HAZEL M. SEAR

HAWTHORN BOOKS, INC.
Publishers / NEW YORK

Library of Congress Catalog Card Number: 74-27904
ISBN 0-8015-6754-8
1 2 3 4 5 6 7 8 9 10

For
Helen and Karolene,
because they asked how.

CONTENTS

I Shirt

II Trousers

III Lined Vest

IV Tie

V Sport Jacket

PREFACE

Why should you buy a book of directions when directions come free with your pattern? Why spend money on information you already have available in other sewing books? Because you'll never find these directions with any pattern, and practically none of this information is in your sewing books.

Prove it? Okay. Look at page 29. Have you ever seen a cuff prepared that way before? Fly zippers? Pages 66–68. Jackets? Pages 96–144.

This book is set up like pattern instructions. That's the easiest way for you to see—and *use*—all this new information. Men's clothing is not difficult to sew if you know how to put it together. With this book you'll learn how—the easy way.

Some of the directions may already be familiar to you. After all, a seam is a seam is a seam. But flip through the book. If you find more familiar than unfamiliar directions, you are truly an expert seamstress, but I guarantee that you will still find something new.

This book is for you if you are tired of sewing shirts that after the first washing have wrinkled collars and cuffs; baggy pants with waistbands that roll over; or jackets that look as though they've been slept in before they are finished.

And if, like most of the women I've talked to, you hesitate to try to make men's clothing because you know how fussy your man can be about his apparel, or because you've tried sewing men's clothes and were unhappy when they came out looking "homemade," or because you think tailoring is too difficult, or you just didn't think you could sew them right; then you've come to the right place.

This book will help you take the "homemade" out of your sewing, show you how to make professional-looking garments, remove the frustration of incomplete or difficult-to-understand directions and, best of all, do these things simply and easily.

The first time someone says in *that* tone of voice: "You didn't REALLY make that jacket, did you?" you'll know why you bought this book.

The Sew-Easy Guide To Menswear

WHAT THIS BOOK WILL SHOW YOU

When my husband decided that he needed a few jackets and lots of pants and shirts, I began looking for the cheapest, simplest, quickest method of fulfilling his requirements without exhausting either myself or our budget. After attending every sewing clinic I could find and applying my own twenty years of sewing experience, I have come up with some new methods that simplify the tricky sewing required for menswear.

Unfortunately, we aren't able to duplicate professional manufacturing methods at home. But we can and do use some of the tricks of the trade.

If you haven't done much sewing, this guide will help you. If you've sewn for years but hesitated on pants and jackets because you thought they would take too long to make or wouldn't look right when they were done, well, do we have a surprise for you! Novice or old hand, this book will show the way. I've made all the mistakes and invented a few of my own. Eliminating them leaves only the best and easiest way to get the job done right.

We will use commercial patterns for the basic garment. I do have comments about detailing those garments: how to change your pattern to give you the effect you desire and how to make permanent patterns. When sewing menswear, remember, every garment is basic. A shirt is a shirt is a shirt. That goes for other clothing as well. So once you have completed a garment that fits properly, you can make any adjustments you'd like to make it fashionable.

This guide gives directions for five garments: shirt, trousers, vest, tie, and sport jacket. We start with a shirt because, if you have sewn at all, the pieces are familiar to you. The trousers, vest, and tie are all comparatively easy. Then, with your confidence at its peak, we hand you the biggie—the sport jacket. By then you should be able to sail right through the jacket without any qualms.

I only explain a particular construction once. For instance, in the shirt section I tell you how to sew a dart. By the time you get to the pants and vest I assume you know how and don't detail the dart again. There are several different styles of pockets included; all you have to do is choose the one you prefer for your garment.

The shirt instructions are for a dress shirt that can be worn to work: one with long sleeves and a neck suitable for wearing a tie (with variations thrown in). The constructions we talk about will be for woven fabrics. Near the end of the shirt chapter you will find notes on knits to help you with knitted fabrics. And for the advanced I have included a few tricks to speed the production.

Since I detail different styles of shirts, trouser pockets, and jackets, check through the instructions first and choose those that apply to your garment. Ignore the rest.

In men's clothing it's the details that make the difference. So watch the details and follow the step-by-step instructions and the garments you make will look professional. (Note also that the tailoring for men's shirts can also be applied to the shirtwaist fashions popular for women.)

Remember, I've thrown out the mistakes. Don't skip any of the steps and be sure to press each stage as you sew. You can't miss.

COMING TO TERMS WITH TERMS

Before we do anything else we must be sure we are speaking the same language. What I mean when I say something and what you think I'm talking about can be two different things, so here are my definitions for the terms. You will also find expanded views of the five garments we are making to help you visualize them better.

BACKSTITCH: used to anchor the seam at the top and bottom. It consists of making several backward stitches immediately before the end of the seam and then sewing forward again over the stitches you have just sewn (see Figure 10).

BASTING: long stitches of a different color of thread used either to mark a sewing detail or to anchor two or three pieces of material together before final stitching. Sometimes used on the finished seam until it is pressed.

BELTING: a stiffener for belts. (If you can, get the type that is flexible. I say, "It's like horsehair braiding," and usually the salesgirl knows what I want. The white, cardboardy type that comes in belt kits is too thick for our purposes.) Belting can also be constructed of several layers of stiffener, interfacing, and bias tape for insertion in trouser waistbands. Usually when I say belting, I mean the belting we make.

BIAS: a line at a 45-degree angle to the selvage (or straight grain). Material cut on the bias stretches, won't ravel, and encourages a smoother fit.

CLIP: cutting a single or double layer of the seam allowance to the stitching on a seam to make a smooth turn or trimming away excess material such as in corners or bulky seams.

FEED DOG: the cleated piece directly beneath the sewing-machine needle that pulls the material through the machine as you sew.

INTERFACING: a firm fabric, woven or nonwoven, placed between two layers of material for stability and body. (We use interfacing in collars, cuffs, in back of facings, for pocket edges, belts, and flys. If you have a covered edge, you will use interfacing.)

There are at least fifty different types of material on the market that can be used for interfacing. I prefer a nonwoven interfacing because it has no bias—so I can lay my pattern pieces in any direction on the interfacing. Sometimes, however, you should use woven interfacings.

Here are my recommendations for interfacing.

Shirt: use lightweight, nonwoven interfacing.

Trousers: lightweight, nonwoven interfacing, except in the belting. Details for the belting are in the trouser section.

Tie: loosely woven interfacing. Tell the salesgirl you are making a tie, and she will sell you the right kind.

Vest: lightweight, nonwoven interfacing.

Jacket: for wools and heavyweight materials, buy the very best heavyweight hair canvas (woven). For medium-weight fabrics, buy medium-weight hair canvas, again the best. For lightweight materials, buy medium-weight hair canvas. Buy lightweight woven interfacing and lightweight nonwoven interfacing for the pockets.

Each section tells you what to use the interfacing for and which pieces to interface.

LINING: a lightweight material used to cover the inner surface of the garment. It is made separately, in one piece, and sewn into the garment with its wrong side against the wrong side of the fabric you are working with.

MATERIAL: the fabric you are using to construct the main body of your garment.

MEASURE: the dimensions of the person you are making garments for. Professionals use cloth or plastic tape measures. I use a flexible steel tape because it never stretches and is always easy to read.

When measuring, do not pull the tape measure tightly against the body. Placing two fingers between the body and the tape measure will keep the measurements closer to normal dimensions. After all, no one stands at attention in his clothes all the time, so make the garments comfortable to wear by giving the wearer a little moving room.

NOTCHES: numbered triangles on the pattern seam allowance used to match one pattern piece to another for proper alignment.

PLACKET: a slit in long shirt-sleeves to make the sleeve easy to put on or take off.

SEAMS: You will sew your pieces together several different ways. These are the seams you will use:

Bound seams: After you sew a straight seam, the raw edges of the seam allowances are covered with bias strips. All the exposed seam allowance edges in the half-lined jacket are bound, usually with the same material you use to line the jacket.

Flat-fell seam: a seam that leaves no raw edges. To sew, put WRONG sides of seam together. Sew the seam on the sewing line. Trim or clip away one seam allowance to within ⅛ or ¼ inch of the seam. Turn the raw edge of the other seam allowance to the stitching. Pin and topstitch the length of the seam. Figures 58 and 94 show the flat-fell seam.

French seam: a seam inside a seam. It is used to cover raw edges where a flat-fell seam is too difficult to sew. To sew, with wrong sides together sew a ¼-inch seam. Press seam open. Turn and press pieces together along the seam. Sew ⅜ inch in from the first seam edge. Figures 148 and 149 show a French seam in the trouser back pocket.

Straight or regular seam: a row of plain stitches along the sewing line.

SEAM ALLOWANCE: ⅝ inch from the cutting line to the stitching line. All seam allowances are ⅝ inch unless otherwise noted.

SEAM RIPPER: a sharp, double-pointed tool with one end longer than the other (it looks like a J with a handle). The short end sometimes has a small ball on it and the curve of the J is razor sharp for cutting.

STRAIGHT GRAIN: the unbroken threads of a woven material. Usually, straight grain means the lengthwise or long threads running the length of your yardage between the selvages, although crosswise threads, from selvage to selvage, are also straight grain.

Material cut on the lengthwise grain does not give or gives very little. It is also very strong. Material cut on the crosswise grain will stretch a little, depending on the weave (a weave of 108 threads per inch will

7

not stretch as much as a weave of 90 threads per inch; the 108-thread weave is very strong and stiff because the threads are packed together).

SEWING LINE: the line inside the seam allowance on each pattern piece. This line is where you make your stitches. Pin and sew on the sewing line to make your clothing fit properly. All of the pattern measurements and styling details are based on the sewing line.

STITCHES: During construction you will have to do some special stitching either by hand or machine. These stitches are:

Padding stitch: a tailoring stitch used on collars and lapels of jackets (described in detail in the jacket section).

Running stitch: a long basting stitch done by hand and used to lightly anchor one piece to another. Figure 366 and Figure 402 show two ways you will use the running stitch.

Slip stitch: regular hemming stitch. With a threaded needle, pick up a couple of threads in the folded edge of the hem, then a couple of threads in the main body of the garment. Return the needle to the fold of the hem and bring it out no more than ½ inch farther along, pulling the needle through.

Stay stitching: a row of machine stitches sewn into the seam allowance above the sewing line. Patterns call for stay stitching in collars, necks, shoulders, sleeves, or any curved seam.

Stay stitching is used to keep the curved edges from stretching out of shape. I don't tell you to stay stitch because you are not asked to handle a piece until you are going to sew it, so you don't run the risk of stretching it out of shape. One exception—if you wish, stay stitch the jacket neck.

Tailor's buttonhole stitch: a special buttonhole stitch that puts a knotted edge on the edge of a buttonhole slash. It wears very well and looks professional, because it is. Figures 424 to 426 explain how to do this stitch.

Topstitch: stitching on the top of the garment, used for decoration or anchoring one piece to another. Some pockets and welts are anchored by topstitching.

TAILORING MARKS: details that are marked on the pattern—such as darts, pockets, center front, that sort of thing. The chalk is used to transfer these tailoring marks to the material.

TAILOR'S CHALK: pencil-like chalk pieces and square wax pieces used to mark the pattern details on the material. The wax usually presses out when you iron over it, and the chalk rubs off easily. Check the wax on a scrap of material to make sure it will disappear; if it won't, use the chalk.

TAILOR'S HAM: a sawdust-stuffed, ham-shaped pillow, one side of cotton, the other of wool. It is used for shaping and pressing curves, as for tailored collars.

TAILOR'S TACKS: thread markings used when other marks might show in the finished garment. Figure 304 shows how to make a tailor tack.

TAPE MEASURE: I use the narrow, flexible, steel variety that has a button to push when you don't want the tape to rewind automatically back into the case. You may use a cloth or plastic tape for body measurements, but they tend to stretch after use.

THREAD: There are many kinds of thread on the market—cotton, polyester, silk, nylon, and cotton-covered polyester. Match your thread to your fabric; sew cotton with cotton, wool with silk. (The polyester is stronger and not as likely to break so I use polyester for everything. But I told you what the experts say.)

One company makes a wax-coated thread. Use it for hand sewing; it is smooth and easy to work with. But if you run it through the machine, the wax builds up on the machine parts, tends to cause drag, and you will have to have the tension parts cleaned to get rid of the wax.

Thread, when spun, is twisted either to the right or left (**Figure 1.**). If you find the thread tangling when you sew by hand, you are going against the twist. Hold up a piece of thread and try to unwind it. Which way do the threads go? If they are right, knot the end of your thread farthest from the spool. If they are left, knot the end by the spool.

Figure 2. If your thread winds on itself when you sew, rotate your needle in the direction opposite the

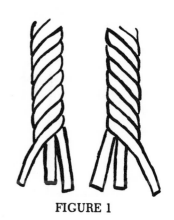

FIGURE 1

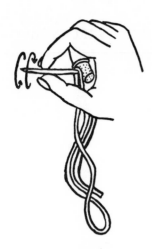

FIGURE 2

twist before each stitch and the thread will not twist. It's difficult at first, but easy after you get used to it.

TWILL TAPE: a woven cotton tape used to keep a seam from stretching. It is used with knits and in tailoring.

VENTS: finished openings at the bottom of jacket sleeves, sides, or back. Sleeve units are decorative; side or back vents on a jacket hem give the garment a smooth appearance while allowing freedom of movement.

WELT: a narrow band of material across the top of a pocket; used as decoration and to give the top of the pocket a bit of body.

YOKE: the fitted piece across the back neck and shoulders in a shirt. We cut two yoke pieces and sandwich the back between them, so there are no raw edges showing in the finished shirt.

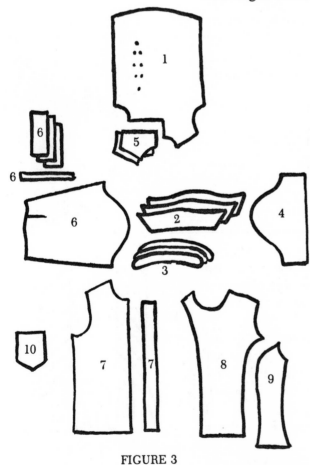

Pattern Pieces
Figure 3. Shirt:
1. Shirt back
2. Undercollar: interfacing; upper collar
3. Band; interfacing; band
4. Short sleeve
5. Yoke
6. Long sleeve; placket facing; cuff; interfacing; cuff
7. Banded shirtfront; band
8. Two-piece shirtfront; interfacing
9. Side piece for two-piece shirtfront
10. Pocket

FIGURE 3

Figure 4. Trousers:
Back Trousers

1. Pocket
2. Facing
3. Welt; interfacing
4. Trouser back
5. Lower part of yoked trouser back
6. Yoke; trouser back
7. Facing
8. Pocket

Belt

1. Loops
2. Belt
3. Belting

Front Trousers

1. Pocket
2. Facing
3. Facing; interfacing
4. Trouser front
5. Fly; interfacing
6. Fly; interfacing
7. Yoked pocket front
8. Pocket yoke
9. Pocket
10. Pocket
11. Facing

FIGURE 4

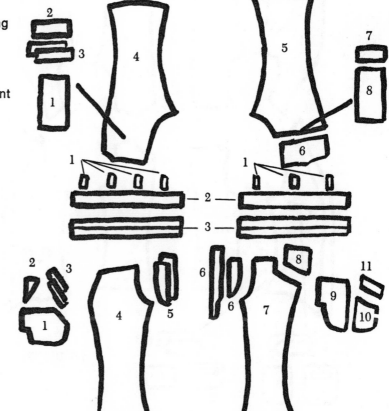

Figure 5. Vest:

1. Vest front lining
2. Vest back lining
3. Upper pocket; welt; interfacing
4. Lower pocket piece for upper pocket
5. Upper pocket piece for upper pocket
6. Lower pocket; welt; interfacing
7. Lower pocket piece for lower pocket
8. Upper pocket piece for lower pocket
9. Vest front; interfacing
10. Vest back
11. Vest back
12. Vest front; interfacing

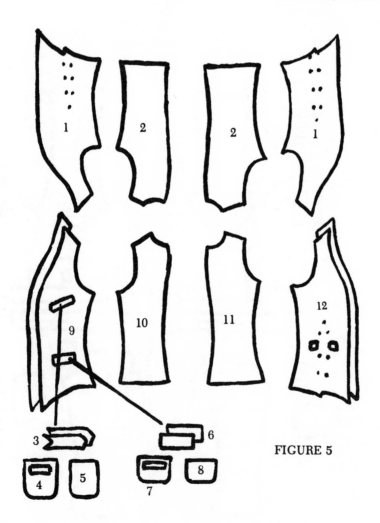

FIGURE 5

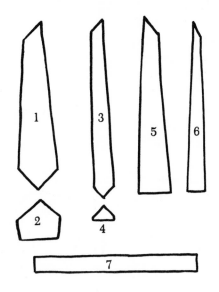

Figure 6. Tie:

1. Large end; tie
2. Large end; lining
3. Small end; tie
4. Small end; lining
5. Large end; interfacing
6. Small end; interfacing
7. Added interfacing

FIGURE 6

Figure 7. Jacket, Outside:

1. Back, with back vent
2. Undersleeve
3. Upper sleeve
4. Side front
5. Front
6. Welt pocket; upper, lower pocket; interfacing
7. Upper collar
8. Undercollar
9. Flap
10. Patch pocket; lining; interfacing
11. Inset pocket; welt; interfacing; upper, lower pocket; interfacing
12. Front
13. Facing
14. Back, side vent

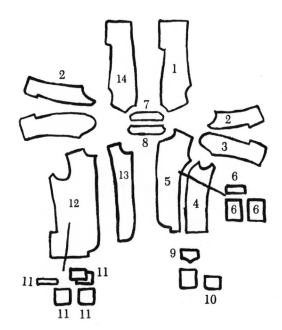

FIGURE 7

Figure 8. Jacket, Interfacing, and Padding:

1. Side vent interfacing
2. Back hem interfacing
3. Back vent interfacing
4. Back interfacing
5. Collar interfacing
6. Shoulder pad
7. Sleeve padding
8. Sleeve interfacing
9. Chest padding
10. Front interfacing
11. Side front interfacing
12. Pocket interfacing
13. Front hem interfacing

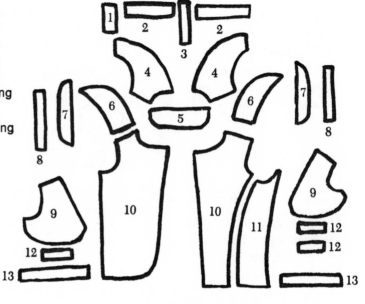

FIGURE 8

Figure 9. Jacket, Lining:

1. Back lining
2. Back vent lining
3. Undersleeve lining
4. Upper sleeve lining
5. Front lining
6. Pocket; interfacing

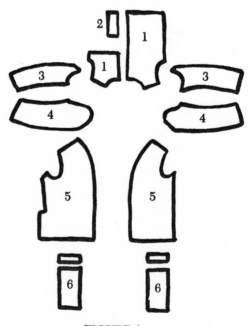

FIGURE 9

FIGURE 10

GENERAL INSTRUCTIONS

There are a few things that you *always* do. Even if I forget to tell you, you shouldn't forget.

ALWAYS:

Clip threads as you go.

Backstitch, **Figure 10,** for permanency. Seams don't pull out if they are backstitched. Or knot, **Figure 11.** Pull the upper thread to the wrong side and bring both threads under the last stitch. Put the threads through the loop and pull tight. Or, **Figure 12,** pull the top thread through and use a square knot to tie thé ends; but be sure to get rid of the ends.

Interface as shown. A simple rule for interfacing: interface all edges. Extra body is essential in collars, cuffs, waistbands, fronts, and flys. Without interfacing the garment won't just wilt—it will collapse—and there go the smooth lines we are striving so hard for.

When in doubt *Press.* Even if I don't tell you, *Press.* (I sometimes tell you to wait but those are the only exceptions.) Manufacturers have special equipment for putting beautiful creases in trousers and for pressing jackets, but we must rely on the iron. Next to the sewing machine the iron is our most important appliance. To press, set the iron on the area to be pressed and let it steam (different materials require different timing; pick up the iron and set it down right next to where it was before. Do not iron as you would a finished garment; you might iron in sags or bulges that you don't want. Just pick the iron up and set it down.

Pin all seams on the sewing line. Only the sport jacket calls for basting, and that's kept to a minimum. (You use basting stiches to indicate tailoring marks because the chalk usually rubs off by the time you reach the next step.) Our object in this book is to do the job as quickly and easily as possible, so pin. As you become familiar with the steps you'll find you use fewer pins, and for some steps you'll use no pins at all. Use pins as shown until you think you can do without.

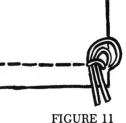

FIGURE 11

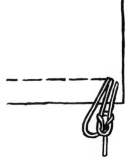

FIGURE 12

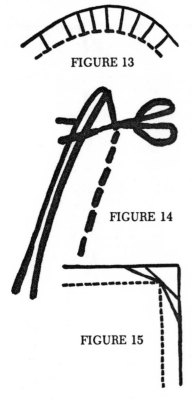

FIGURE 13

FIGURE 14

FIGURE 15

Clip curved seams and corners. Either as in **Figure 13**, cut to the seam line, or as in **Figure 14**, fold the seam allowance and cut. But, *please!* Don't cut past the stitches.

You can reinforce *Corners* by restitching, as close as possible to the first row of stitches, using a smaller stitch for one inch to the corner and one inch past the corner, or by going back and stitching over the first row of stitches for one inch on both sides of the corner. Cut an angle from the corner, as shown in **Figure 15**. Cut another angle along the lines shown across the seams.

Finger Press curved seams and short seams where you can't use the iron without creasing another part of the piece. This method is for seams where a knife-edge is desired: collars, cuffs, etc. Open the seam and put both thumbs on the seam with your first fingers underneath as in **Figure 16**. Hold the seam with thumb 2; run the thumbnail of thumb 1 along the seam, using the finger as a board. The arrow shows direction and length of movement. Move thumb 2 until it is next to thumb 1 and move thumb 1 again until you reach the end of the seam.

To *Turn* a corner, **Figure 17**, put a thumb into the corner as far as possible. With a finger on the corner, push down to the thumb and turn the piece over your finger. Your corner will then look like **Figure 18**. Use a crochet hook or knitting needle to push the corner out, being careful not to put a hole in the fabric.

FIGURE 16

FIGURE 17

FIGURE 18

Roll the seam you finger press and the corners you turn. Holding the seam as shown in **Figure 19,** move the thumbs and fingers up and down until both sides of the piece are even. If any material overlaps, make that the top side. Pin as shown in **Figure 20.** The back side should be pulled down a bit more before it is pinned, as in **Figure 21.** To press, don't put the iron down; just hold it over the seam and let the steam work for you.

FIGURE 19

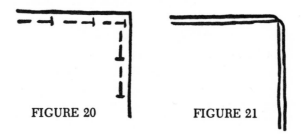

FIGURE 20   FIGURE 21

Notches, **Figure 22,** are indications on the pattern pieces showing where two pieces fit together. On shirts always cut the notches away from the seam line rather than into the seam allowance since we sew flat-fell seams where an inward notch can be disastrous (**Figure 23**).

Notch the back center of the shirt on the collar, band, yoke, and shirt back; front fold line on both the top and bottom of both shirtfronts, and the center of the sleeves and on the yoke where the top of the sleeve is positioned (**Figure 24**).

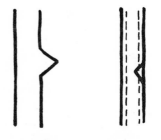

FIGURE 22   FIGURE 23

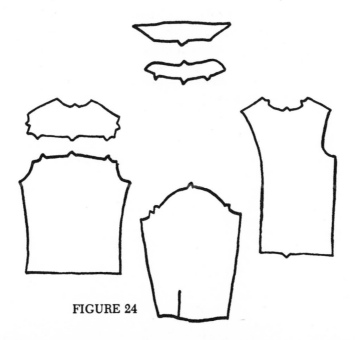

FIGURE 24

As important as cutting and sewing, fitting can make or break a garment. This book gives a few easy pattern adjustments you can make as you go along to ensure proper fit in the shirt, trousers, and vest.

Fitting a jacket is a horse of a different color. In the back of the book you will find a listing of sewing books that detail the fitting procedure.

To make it easier to get a really good fit in the first place, do yourself a favor and buy an expensive pattern. With an expensive pattern you are buying not only style but fit. Fitting takes time. Pattern manufacturers can't take the time to make better fitting patterns unless you are willing to pay a higher price for the pattern. It's false economy to buy a cheaper pattern and spend a lot of time and effort making a trial garment when the better pattern will have a good fit to start with. Don't be reluctant to buy an expensive pattern, you won't regret the extra expense.

Then, don't be lulled into a sense of false security because you bought an expensive pattern. Skipping the muslin trial garment (a jacket shell made out of muslin and basted together to make pattern adjustments) is a luxury you can't afford. You are spending a great deal of money for materials and using your valuable time to make a good-looking garment. Don't waste your expenditures; take the extra day to make the trial garment to get the pattern to fit right. Extra effort now will save you disappointment later, and the next time you will have a pattern that fits without any fuss.

In the jacket section I tell you when to make your trial garment. Have your list of adjustments handy and do a good job. Sewing the jacket the second time will be easier and you won't make mistakes in your expensive material.

Now that I've armed you with information, let's take the plunge.

1 SHIRT

BEFORE WE BEGIN

Keep plenty of pins on hand. You can never have too many. Set up your iron and board. Never sew without pressing; it makes a bigger difference in the tailored look of your garment than any other single process. Thread 'your sewing machine with thread that matches your fabric. If you can't match the thread exactly, use a darker color on top and a lighter color in the bobbin. Buttons: I like the 7/16s for shirts but often 9/16s are the only ones available. White are good on anything, even the dark colors.

GETTING STARTED

Careful measurements are a must for proper fit. Measure his neck around the base of the neck. Measure his chest, as high under the armpits as you can, making sure that the tape measure goes over the shoulder blades and doesn't dip or sag. For back length, measure from the big bone at the base of the neck to the waist. For arm length, tell him to crook his arm to the side a little below shoulder height; measure from the big bone at the neck base to the sharp bone in the shoulder, down the back of the arm to the elbow, and around to the wrist.

Commercial patterns for men are sized by chest measurement. Buy the pattern that is closest to his measurement. If his chest is 40½, I'd buy a 40. Men's patterns are bigger on the average than women's, and men don't mind being called a 40 if that is what they are. When you get the pattern home, measure it for chest size: twice across the back (from center back to side seam) and from the center front to the side seam, also twice. The measurement should equal his chest size plus one inch moving room. For a 40-inch chest the pattern should measure 41 inches. If you feel the pattern chest measurement is not going to be enough, keep your seams ¼ inch smaller than the ⅝ inch allowed, or cut an extra ¼ inch around the outside of the pattern on the side and front seams.

My husband's arms are 3 inches longer than any pattern manufacturer thinks it's possible to have, so I lengthen his sleeves by 3 inches. Most patterns call for approximately 2¾ yards of 45-inch material for a long-sleeved shirt. I buy 3 yards and use the extra for shirttail, longer sleeves, and two pockets. The new, fitted shirts don't have any pockets, but styling details are up to you.

Carry a list of yardages with you when you go shopping. Sales crop up and you'll be able to take advantage of the savings on shirt material.

SHIRT SHOPPING LIST

Pattern
Material
Interfacing
Buttons
Matching thread

CUTTING THE BASIC SHIRT

Lay the shirt out as shown in your pattern cutting illustration. Most commercial patterns have straight shirttails. If you want a longer tail for easier tucking, you'll have to lengthen it. Measure 6 inches below the back (front, too, if you like) and pin a curved line to the side seam (**Figure 25**). I have found that lengthening the back tail is sufficient.

FIGURE 25

Cuff
cut 4

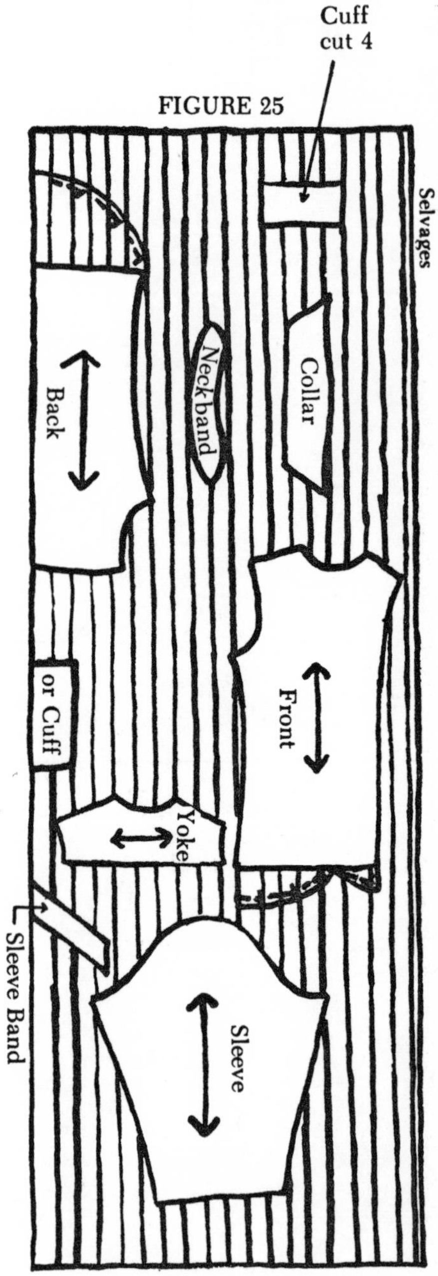

Do not use as a cutting layout;
for illustration purposes only.

Fashion today decrees that men's shirts have two-button cuffs, so cut the cuff ½ inch longer. French cuffs are double the regular cuff. If the pattern on the yoke is to run vertically, the same as the body of the shirt, the yoke must be laid on the up-and-down or crosswise grain. See Figure 25 again. Collar and cuffs may be the same (vertical) or horizontal. Decide for yourself which you prefer. For bias collars in plaids, lay the top collar on the bias.

The easiest way to make sure your shirts are stylish is to keep an eye on newspaper and magazine advertising. When you shop, check the shirts to see what's new. By altering the way you cut the pattern, you can keep your shirts in style.

Banded Collar

Measure around the neck of your shirt pattern on the sewing line of the front and yoke. Measure your collar inside the sewing line. The measurements have to be the same.

To make the collar fit your shirt neck, fold the collar pattern in half. Fold it in half again and cut it apart on the second fold. Lay the collar piece on tissue paper and widen or narrow it along the two cuts—adding or removing half of the desired amount on each side.

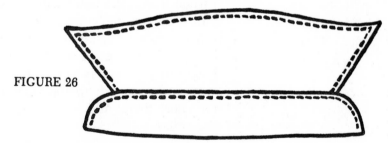

FIGURE 26

Figure 26. There are two popular kinds of shirt collars—banded, such as the ones on most ready-to-wear dress shirts (Figure 26) and sport collars (Figure 29), which are soft, one-piece collars.

Banded collars are preferable on dress shirts because they have more shape. If your pattern has the same lines as the collar in Figure 26, it is simple to make a banded collar out of it. Your band should be 1½ to 1¾ inches longer than his neck measurement.

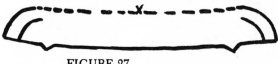

FIGURE 27

Figure 27. Fold the pattern in half. Measure 1½ inches up from the sewing line at the fold and make a mark. That is the top of your band. Draw a very slight downward curve from the mark to where the curved line and the straight part of the collar meet. Cut the collar apart on that line. If you keep the pattern folded, both sides will be the same. Remember to add ⅝ inch seam allowance to the top of the band.

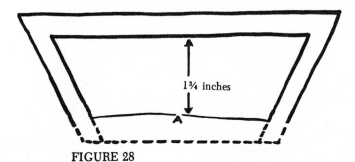

FIGURE 28

Figure 28. Pin the collar piece on tissue paper. The collar must be at least ¼ inch longer, from the neck to the outer edge, than the band. When the collar is turned down, the band will not show and the collar will cover the neck seam.

Measure your collar along the center line. A 1½-inch band will require a 1¾-inch collar. Mark the correct length of your collar at A. Draw a line from A to the sides. Add ¼ inch to the sides if your collar looks too short there. Add ⅝ inch seam allowance. Cut out the collar.

Sport Collar

If your pattern has a sport collar you must convert it to a banded collar if you wish to sew a dress shirt. Sport collars are smaller than the shirt neck measurement. See page 21 for directions to widen the sport collar.

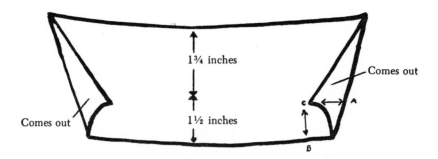

FIGURE 29

Figure 29. Cut away the seam allowance all around the pattern. Fold the collar in half. Measure 1½ inches up from the back center of the collar, or the desired amount for your band. Measure one inch up from the corner along the side seam to point A. Measure one inch along the bottom to point B. Draw a straight line into the collar from point A. Draw a straight line up the collar from point B. The lines will meet at point C. Draw a smooth curve from point C to the lower corner of the collar. Draw a curve from the center back to point C. Draw a straight line from point C to the upper corner of your collar. Cut out the band. Cut off the excess on the side of the collar.

Place the band on paper and trace around it. Add ⅝ inch seam allowance all around the band.

Pin the collar piece to tissue paper, make your center back line 1¼ inches longer than your band. Lengthen the sides ¼ inch. Draw a smooth line across the bottom. Add ⅝ inch seam allowance on the bottom, sides, and top. Figures 27 and 28 show what your two pieces should look like. Cut out the collar.

Now check back to Figure 24. Cut a notch on the yoke where the pattern says "center sleeve here." Cut another notch on the center top of the sleeve, and on the fold line—top and bottom—of the shirtfronts. Not the center line, but the FOLD line. For the casual long sleeve placket, cut two bias strips, each 1½ inches wide and twice the length of the long-sleeve slash; these will be your plackets. The bias strips sew much more easily than straight pieces.

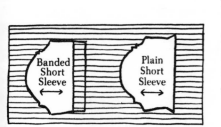

FIGURE 30
Do not use as a cutting layout;
for illustration purposes only.

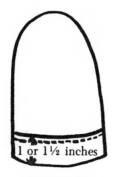

FIGURE 31

For the dress placket cut a 3-inch strip on the straight grain, the length of·one side of the placket plus 2 inches. Cut a 1-inch-wide strip the length of one side of the placket plus 1 inch; this piece is also straight grain.

Cut out the pockets. If you wish to reinforce them for extra durability, cut four.

Cut interfacing pieces for collar (two pieces of interfacing make a nice stiff collar), neckband, cuffs, and front facing. Do not interface the plackets. The bias strip won't work for you, and the dress placket will be too stiff.

Short Sleeves

Cut a plain short sleeve, adding a small flare to the hem allowance, if the pattern doesn't have any, to ensure that the circumference of the hem won't be smaller than that of the sleeve, which would cause puckering (**Figure 30**). On banded shirt-sleeves cut an extra 1 or 1½ inches, depending on where you want the band to fall on the sleeve (**Figure 30** and **Figure 31**).

Banded Shirtfront

Fold the facing to the fold line. For the right side, cut only 1½ inches of the facing; if you cut the facing off the pattern, you won't be able to use the pattern for a plain-front shirt. On the left, fold pattern on fold line and cut along the fold line. Cut a band 2 inches wide for the left side. These bands are often bias. (Figures 50 to 54 show you how to put them together and will give you a better idea of what to cut.)

Now it's all cut out and we're ready to sew.

NOTE: Where you have two pieces (pockets, cuffs, sleeves, etc.), repeat the directions given the first time.

SEWING THE BASIC SHIRT

Separate the collar, neckband, cuffs, and pockets from the rest of the pattern pieces. We make these first so, when we are putting the shirt together, we don't have to stop and construct the piece we need next.

Making the Pocket

Figure 32. Fold on the sewing line all around the pocket and pin.

FIGURE 32

Figure 33. Fold the pocket in half to make sure it is even. Adjust your pins until it is. Press, holding the iron above the pocket without touching, or the pin marks will show. Remove pins on top and stitch across the top of the pocket. Press.

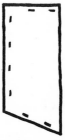

FIGURE 33

Figure 34. Fold flap down, making pocket desired depth, and sew as close to the bottom edge as you can.

FIGURE 34

Figure 35. Dress shirt pockets look like this. Follow above directions but curve your stitching line.

If you want a two-pocket shirt, make the second pocket to match the first.

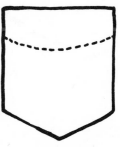

FIGURE 35

25

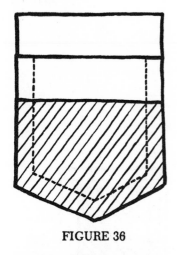

FIGURE 36

Figure 36. Then there are reinforced, or double, pockets. (Remember that for a reinforced pocket you cut two pieces of fabric for each pocket.) Lay the pieces with right sides together. Turn the top of one side down to the desired depth. Stitch as shown around the sides and the bottom. Clip the corners (Figure 15).

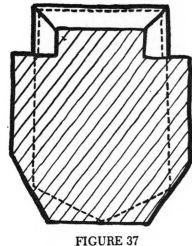

FIGURE 37

Figure 37. Turn the pocket over, clip the top of the unsewn piece to the stitch line, and sew a narrow hem on the sides and top of the extending flap. Finger press the seams. Turn the pocket right side out.

Figure 38. Turn the flap over the opening and stitch across about one inch from the hemmed edge.

Collar

Figure 39. Cut ¼ inch from the sides, top, and bottom of the undercollar. Fit your collar pieces together this way: interfacing on the bottom; upper collar,

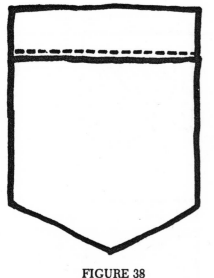

FIGURE 38

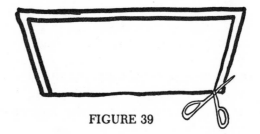

FIGURE 39

right side up; undercollar, right side facing upper collar. Sew with the undercollar up. The feed dog will take up the extra material in the upper collar and the interfacing, so they do fit together. *Do not pin.* (Don't worry. Everything works out.)

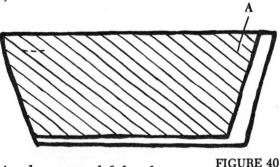

A

FIGURE 40

Figure 40. Begin stitching in the upper left-hand corner of the long seam. Gently pull the undercollar as you sew (the feed dog takes up that ¼ inch). Sew to point A.

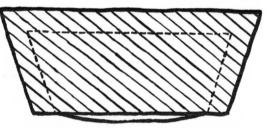

FIGURE 41

Figure 41. Match sides and sew down the left. Pull the collar gently and sew the right side. Don't forget to tie off all thread ends. Spread the seam and run your finger along both the inside and outside. Inch along the seam until it stays open (finger press). Clip the corners as close to the stitching as possible. Clip the top seam allowances.

Turn the collar. Use a crochet hook to push out the corners. Roll the top of the collar between your fingers until the edge is smooth and even. When you look at the top collar, no undercollar should show. Pin as you go.

Figure 42. Any excess collar should show on the underside. Press, gently pulling the collar to help it keep its shape. Remove the pins and press again.

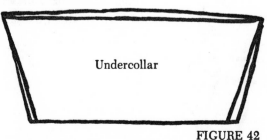

Undercollar

FIGURE 42

When the undercollar is cut shorter, the upper collar is pulled over the seam, leaving a smooth finish. After washing, the collar will still retain this smoothness without the wrinkles that normally develop in "homemade" clothes. The wrinkles are caused because, when the undercollar is turned, it has a little more material in it than the upper collar. Eliminate the excess material and you eliminate the wrinkles.

If you are making a sport collar, skip to the cuffs.

Collarband

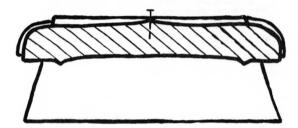

FIGURE 43

Figure 43. Pin the middle of the collar and the neckband pieces together. Pull the undercollar down to match the edge of the upper collar. The undercollar will be tighter, so when the collar is turned down— no wrinkles. The notches for attaching the band to the shirt neck will be toward the top of the collar.

Pin the neckband to the collar. Start in the middle and work to the end. The band is cut on the bias and will stretch to fit.

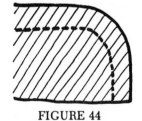

FIGURE 44

Figure 44. Stitching carefully, make a gentle curve. Remove the pins before you sew over them.

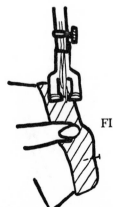

FIGURE 45

Figure 45. Keep one finger on the collarband to smooth the excess away from the needle. When you reach the end you will have more material on top. Cut away the excess. Clip the seam, turn, and press.

28

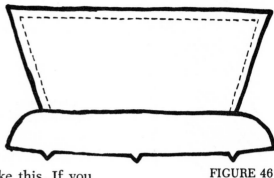

FIGURE 46

Figure 46. Your collar should look like this. If you wish, topstitch the collar now, ¼ inch from the edge, smoothing it as you sew. *Do not* topstitch the band; that comes later.

Put the collar aside.

Making the Cuffs

Figure 47. Turn a little more than one-half of the seam allowance of the top cuff over the top edge of the interfacing. Stitch ¼ inch down from the top. Cut the interfacing bottom to match the cuff piece.

Cut ¼ inch of seam allowance all around the other piece of the cuff.

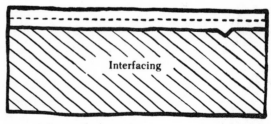

Interfacing

FIGURE 47

Sew as you did the collar (both sides and bottom) pulling the lower cuff piece to match the top. Finger press the seam, clip the corners, and turn. Roll the edges, pinning as you go. Press. Remove the pins and press again. The lower cuff will be longer than the top piece.

Set the cuffs aside.

Now we can put the shirt together without any interruptions.

29

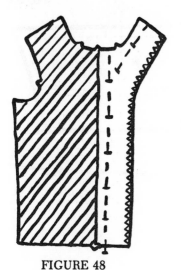

FIGURE 48

Front

Figure 48. Pin the interfacing to the shirtfront keeping the pins well away from the seam line. Sew, using a zigzag stitch, on the edge. You won't get annoying threads after washing, and the front of the shirt will be smooth. Remove the pins and press. Zigzag across the top of the facing for the sport collar finish.

FIGURE 49

Figure 49. Turn the facing on the fold line. (Remember those two notches we cut? Use them as a guide to turn the facing.) Press. This facing is used for both banded and sport collars.

Banded Shirtfront

Figure 50. Lay the right side of the band against the wrong side of the left shirtfront. Pin and sew down the front. Remove pins.

Figure 51. Press the seam toward the side seam. At the same time, fold and press down a ½-inch hem at the outer edge of the band, keeping it straight and even.

FIGURE 50

FIGURE 51

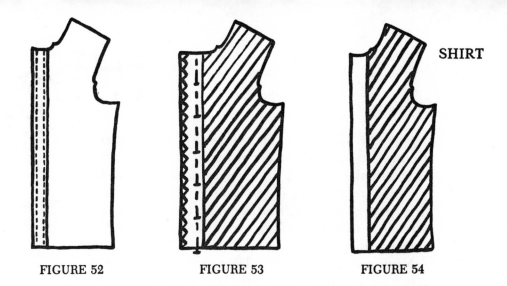

FIGURE 52   FIGURE 53   FIGURE 54

SHIRT

Figure 52. Turn band over the front of the shirt. Pin. Topstitch ¼ inch in from the folded edge down each side of the band. Remove pins and press.

Figure 53. The right side of the banded front usually has a modified facing. Interface it, pin, and zigzag along the edge.

Figure 54. Turn the facing on the fold line and press.

Fitted Shirt, Side Front

Figure 55. Fitted shirts have a piece sewn to the side of the front. Fit *wrong* sides together and pin at the notches. The curve from the top notch will stretch (bias again), so stretch and pin. Pin below the other notch.

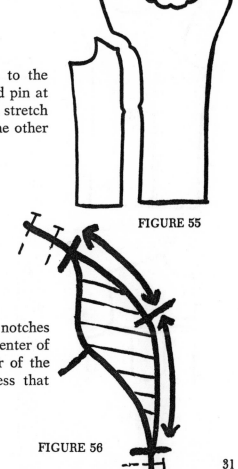

FIGURE 55

Figure 56. To ease the fabric between the notches and to avoid puckering, bring the line in the center of the side front down to the line in the center of the shirtfront and pin. Keep dividing the fullness that results, and pin.

FIGURE 56

31

Figure 57. This is how the seam will look on the side front. Now go back and pin again on the dotted lines. If you think one of the little bulges is too big, pull the pins on either side of it and redistribute the fullness. The curve of the shirtfront is cut on the bias and will stretch to take a lot of the curve, so use as much of it as you can.

Now, you must make a decision. If you sew with the eased side down, your feed dog will help take out the excess material in the side, but you run the risk of sewing puckers into the seam. If you sew with the eased side up, you can smooth the fabric in front of the needle, thus keeping the seam smooth and puckerless. Sew your seam the way you think will be best.

Sew, taking the full seam allowance. Remove the pins and press.

FIGURE 57

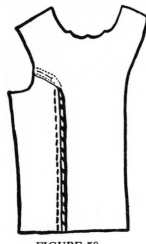

FIGURE 58

Figure 58. Finish the seam as a flat-fell seam by trimming ¼ inch from the seam allowance of the side front, and turning under a ¼-inch hem of the seam allowance of the shirtfront. Then turn the entire seam allowance of the shirtfront down so that it covers the trimmed edge. Topstitch as close as possible to the edge, making sure that your ¼-inch hem doesn't creep out, exposing a raw edge.

Attaching the Pockets

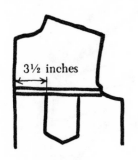

3½ inches

FIGURE 59

Figure 59. Lay a yardstick across the shirtfront, even with the sleeve notch, and pin along the top of the yardstick. With the facing turned, measure 3½ inches in from the fold. Put a pin in vertically. Eyeball the vertical pin. If it seems too close to the edge, move it toward the armhole. The upper inside corner of the pocket goes in the angle of the pins.

Figure 60. Pin the pocket to the shirtfront. Starting at the pocket hem, stitch to the top of the pocket slanting in toward the middle of the pocket—but just a touch! Leaving the needle in the shirt, pivot, take two or three stitches across the top. Leaving the needle in the fabric, pivot again. Stitch along the pocket as close to the edge as you can. Stitch to the top of the pocket on the other side. Pivot, sew two or three stitches, pivot, and slant down to the hem.

Sewing the pockets this way prevents them from tearing out, even with 997 pencils and one pen crammed into them.

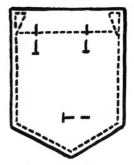

FIGURE 60

Back

Figure 61. If your back has a dart, mark it now. Stick pins in the dots for the dart. Carefully remove the pins holding the pattern to the material. (I usually use those pins to mark the dart, thus killing two birds.) Holding the point of the first pin underneath, gently pull the pattern. It will come away easily, leaving a small hole. Continue in this manner until the pattern is removed and the pins mark the perimeter of the dart.

FIGURE 61

Figure 62. Turn the back over and insert pins next to those already there. Place the second pin as close as possible to the hole made by the first pin.

Figure 63. Open the back and pin the darts. The dotted line is to remind you to keep the dart on the straight grain of your material.

FIGURE 62

FIGURE 63

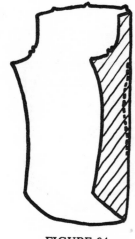

FIGURE 64

Figure 64. Sew the dart. To sew a dart, sew between three and five stitches on the edge of the material above the first pin. Sew as close as you can without going off the edge. As you reach the first pin, sew the dart. At the last pin, again sew three to five stitches close to the edge.

When you remove the pins and press the darts, you will find that those stitches eliminate the cup-shaped puckers normally seen at the ends of darts in home-made clothes.

FIGURE 65

Figure 65. Sandwich the back between the two yoke pieces. Pin together, starting with a pin at the middle and one at each end. Finish pinning as shown. Stitch. Remove pins. Turn back to wrong side.

FIGURE 66

Figure 66. Press, the under yoke piece up. Turn again and pull gently on the upper yoke as you press up until the two pieces match.

Figure 67. Topstitch the yoke about ⅛ inch from the edge if you like.

FIGURE 67

The Body

Figure 68. Pin each shirtfront to the under yoke— the right side of the yoke to the wrong side of the front.

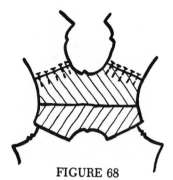

FIGURE 68

Figure 69. If you are sewing a banded collar, the facing is pinned with the front.

FIGURE 69
Front-banded Collar

Figure 70. If you are sewing a sport collar, the facing is not sewn into the yoke.

Sew. Remove pins and press the seams toward the shirt back.

FIGURE 70
Front Sport Collar

Figure 71. Lay the shirt on an ironing board and press the upper yoke over the seam. Press a ⅝-inch hem in the yoke. Pin your seam so the bottom stitching is covered and the yoke lies flat. Topstitch as close to the edge as possible and press.

FIGURE 71

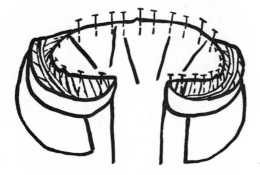

FIGURE 72

Figure 72. On the outside of the shirt, pin the under-side of the band to the shirt, right sides together. Pin the center back and both notches. Pulling gently, pin the rest of the band. The end of the band and the shirtfront must meet *exactly*. If the band is too long, resew the band curve until it matches the front. Sew, being very careful not to catch the fullness of the shirt in your seam and cause puckers.

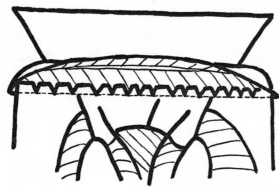

FIGURE 73

Figure 73. Clip the seam. Press it toward the collar.

Figure 74. Press the inner band down, pinning as you go. Make sure the lower stitches are covered by the hem. Sew carefully so the fullness of the shirt is not caught in the stitching. Topstitch around the band.

Isn't that beautiful?

FIGURE 74

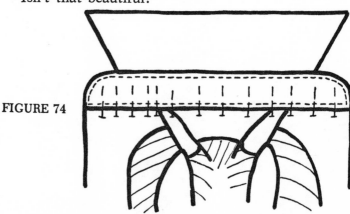

Sport Collar

This is really easy.

Figure 75. With right sides together, pin undercollar to shirt from center back to front. Now bring the upper collar to the neck edge, just to the shoulder

FIGURE 75

seam. Pin. Turn facing over collar and pin shirt, under-collar, upper collar, interfacing, and facing all together just to the end of the facing. Clip the upper collar at the edge of the facing on both sides. Pin the upper collar out of the way. Sew, remove pins, and clip the seam.

Figure 76. Press the seam up toward the collar. Unpin the upper collar, turn a hem under, and cover the stitching, pinning as you go. Sew the upper collar. Bring your stitching one inch past the ends of the fac-ing. Slip stitch the top of the facing to the under yoke.

There is your collar. If you want to topstitch it, start at one bottom edge and sew all the way around.

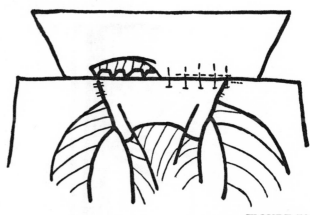

FIGURE 76

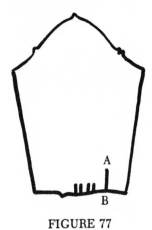

FIGURE 77

Casual Long Sleeve Plackets

Before the long sleeves are sewn into the shirt you sew in the plackets.

Figure 77. Mark your tucks with tailoring chalk (pins usually fall out). Slit your placket from point B to point A.

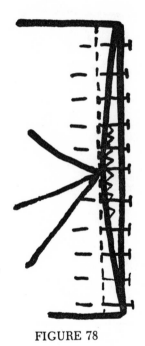

FIGURE 78

Figure 78. Open the placket. Match the ends of the opening to the ends of the bias strip, the right side of the bias to the wrong side of the sleeve. Pin the ends and gently pull open the slit. The point or middle of the slit will not match the bias edge, but will fall almost ½ inch in from the edge. Pin to the bias in a straight line. The edge of the slit will make a very shallow angle from the ends to the middle.

Stitch, making a ½-inch seam from the end of the shirt to the top of the placket and back down to the end of the sleeve. The stitching will be straight on the bias strip but angled on the sleeve.

Figure 79. Zigzag over the straight stitching two inches along the middle of the placket. Catch the threads where the seam is the smallest. I have never had a placket tear loose at this point since I started doing them this way. Remove pins. Press seam toward the placket. Turn the raw edge of the bias over to meet the seam edge. Press.

Figure 80. Turn bias to cover the first row ot stitch ing. Pin and sew, removing the pins as you go. Keep your stitching as close to the edge as possible.

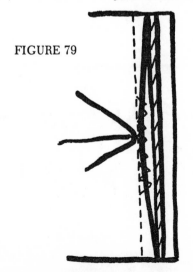

FIGURE 79

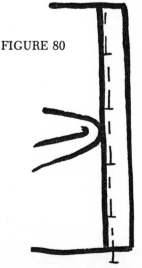

FIGURE 80

Figure 81. Anchor your placket this way: fold it in half and sew a double row of stitches at an angle across the top, or . . .

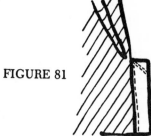

FIGURE 81

Figure 82, this way. Turn the side with the tucks under and stitch across the top of the opening.

FIGURE 82

Dress Long Sleeve Plackets

Now for the dress placket.

Slit the placket opening. Mark the tucks with tailoring chalk.

Figure 83. Pin the narrow strip, right side to the wrong side of the shirt, on the short side of the placket—the one nearest the sleeve seam edge. Sew from the top of the placket down. Leave the inch at the top unstitched and bring it to the right side of the sleeve.

FIGURE 83

Figure 84. Press the seam toward the placket and fold down a narrow hem. Press.

Figure 85. Turn the strip to the outside, cover the first row of stitches, pin, and sew from the top down.

The top will still be unstitched.

FIGURE 84

FIGURE 85

FIGURE 86

Figure 86. On the raw edge of the placket, lay the wide strip on the wrong side of the shirt, right side down. The right side of the strip will be facing the wrong side of the sleeve. Pin and sew. Remove the pins and press the seam toward the placket. Turn and press down a narrow hem on the outer edge of the strip.

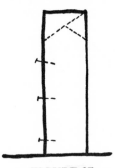

FIGURE 87

Figure 87. Bring the wide strip to the right side of the sleeve. With the placket closed, turn the wide strip to cover the seam you just made. Pin to the top of the placket just to cover the stitches. The unpinned side covers the narrow bound side of the placket. Fold the top as shown by the dotted lines.

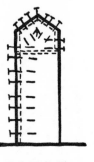

FIGURE 88

Figure 88. Be sure the free end of the small placket is under your triangle. Cut the tail if it is too long. Pin the rest of the placket as shown. Stitch along the pinned side, around the triangle, and twice across the top of the placket. Be sure the top of the slash is above those two sets of horizontal stitches.

Setting in the Sleeves

Figure 89. Pin the sleeve to the body of the shirt *wrong sides together*, matching notches on the body and the yoke. The ends of the shirt should be even with the ends of the sleeve. Pull gently and the sleeve and shirt will stretch to fit. Both the shirt and sleeve are cut on the bias at this point and will stretch nicely. Pin.

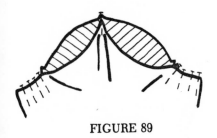

FIGURE 89

Figure 90. With fingers between the shirt and sleeve as shown, run the thumbs to the middle of the space and hold for pinning. The loops will be next to the fingers.

This is an easy method for locating the center points of the loose fabric between the pinned notches

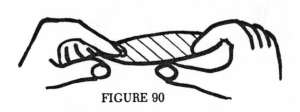

FIGURE 90

of the sleeve and the body of the shirt. When these two center points are pinned together, you have equal amounts of fabric on either side of the pin. This process is similar to the one used on page 31 for making a fitted shirt. See Figures 56 and 57.

Figure 91. This is what your sleeve looks like.

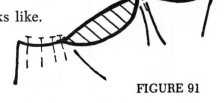

FIGURE 91

Figure 92. Keep reducing your fullness in this manner until the sleeve is completely pinned. Take your time here and you will not have any puckers in the finished seam. Don't be afraid to use plenty of pins. Sew over the pins, taking the full seam allowance.

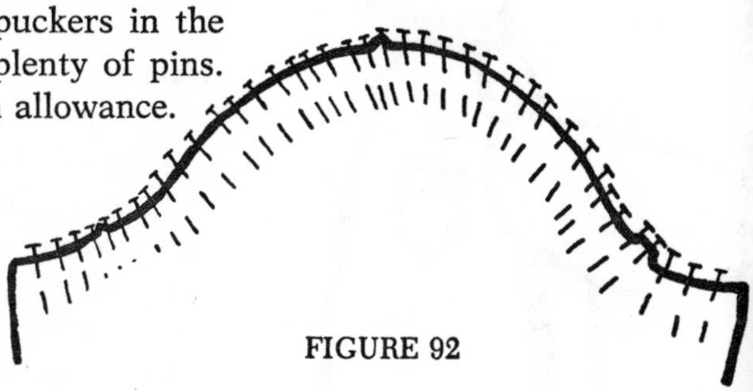

FIGURE 92

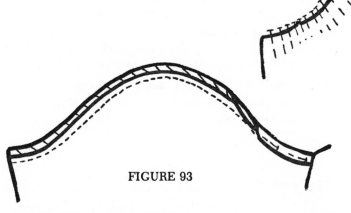

FIGURE 93

Figure 93. Remove the pins. Press the seam toward the sleeve. Clip the sleeve seam allowance close to the stitching. Turn the shirt seam allowance down to the stitching. Pin as shown. Removing pins as you sew, stitch as close to the edge as possible. It can be tricky, so don't sew too fast. This is a flat-fell seam.

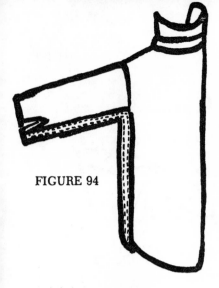

FIGURE 94

Side Seams

Figure 94. Pin the shirt sides and sleeve seams wrong sides together, matching notches. Sew from the end of the sleeve to the hem edge of the shirt on the sewing line. Trim the seam allowance away from the back side and sleeve seams on both sides. Fold the raw edge of the uncut seam allowance to the seam and pin. Make sure your fold is to the back on both sides. Use a rolled-up magazine to pin the sleeve. Stitch from the bottom hem to the end of the sleeve; make sure you keep the rest of the sleeve and shirt out of the way. Cut your threads and press.

Hem

If you'd like to reinforce the side seam of the shirt, cut two 1½-inch squares of material. Fold each square into a triangle. Set them aside but keep them handy. This only works if your shirt has both front and back curved tails; it's also the only place it's necessary.

Figure 95. Turn the front facing inside out as shown. On the bottom, stitch to the end of the facing, taking the entire seam allowance.

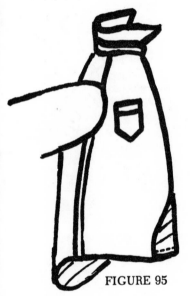

FIGURE 95

Figure 96. On the inside of the shirt, turn one-half of the allowance you made when sewing the facing and sew all around the bottom of the shirt. The curve of the tails turns in quite readily. Keep your fingers turning the hem about 3 or 4 inches in front of the needle. Don't go too fast or you might lose the hem— or a finger.

Figure 97. Position the first raw edge of the triangle with the middle point at the side seam. Pin the raw edge of the triangle even with the raw edge of the

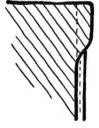

FIGURE 96

42

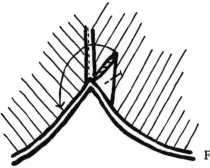

FIGURE 97

shirt hem. The arrow shows where the other point of the triangle will fall after the shirt hem is turned for final stitching.

Figure 98. Turn your facing so it lies flat and is in its correct position. Stitch up from the bottom of the shirt to where the hem begins. Lift the presser foot, pivot fabric around the needle, and sew hem, turning as before, to the triangle tip. Leave needle in shirt. Lift presser foot and turn shirt.

FIGURE 98

Figure 99. Bring the other raw edge of the triangle to the hem, as shown by the arrow in Figure 97. Pin. Turn hem over edge and continue sewing. Place other triangle at other side seam and sew as above. Finish other front the same as you started.

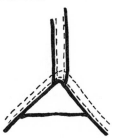

FIGURE 100

FIGURE 99

Figure 100. Turn shirt over and stitch the edge of the hem down across the triangles.

Short Sleeve Finishes—Plain Hem and Banded Hem

Figure 101. For a plain hem, turn up the sleeve to where the flare is narrowest. Turn the raw edge under for a finished edge; pin, hem, and sew.

A banded hem is the finish used on little boys' sleeves and men's shirts when they have a banded front. It's not difficult to do, just hard to explain.

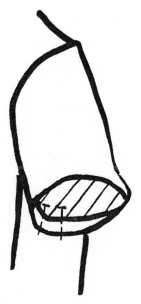

FIGURE 101

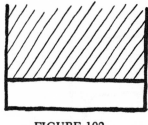

FIGURE 102

Figure 102. Turn under 1 inch and pin.

Figure 103. Turn that hem again in the same direction. Pin ⅜ inch from the edge. When you turn the double hem down, the bottom of the hem becomes the top of the band as seen in **Figure 104.**

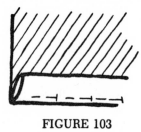

FIGURE 103

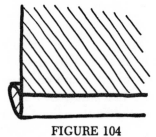

FIGURE 104

FIGURE 105

Figure 105. Pin, and stitch on the outside.

When you finish a shirt with a straight seam, not the flat-fell seam (which is shown in Figure 94), make this sleeve hem before you sew the sleeve into the shirt.

Attaching Cuffs to Long Sleeves

Figure 106. Pin the right side of the bottom or unstitched cuff to the inside of the sleeve, as follows:

Start pinning from the bottom of the placket, the side nearest the side seam; match notches; now fold the top placket toward the side seam and pin. Any fullness left is made into tucks with the outside fold placed toward the top placket. Pin.

For the dress placket, pin both the bottom and top plackets to the cuff, matching the sides of the cuff. Match the notch. Either ease the resulting fullness as you did for the top of the sleeve or make two tucks as shown in Figure 106.

The side cuff seam allowance of the bottom cuff will be pinned, and the seam allowance of the top cuff

FIGURE 106

will be free. Keep the edge of the sleeve even with the edge of the cuff. Sew. Remove the pins and press the sleeve allowance into the cuff.

Figure 107. To turn evenly, the edges of the front cuff must be unsewn past the stitching you just made. Open the side seams of the cuff for at least ½ inch. Figure 107 shows one cuff side with the cuff seam opened down to the cuff-sleeve stitching.

FIGURE 107

Figure 108. Bring the top cuff up over the seam. Pin across. Stitch as close to the edge as possible, keeping parallel with the seam you sewed when you made the cuffs.

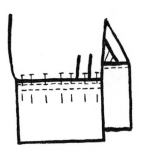

FIGURE 108

Buttonholes

Figure 109. Buttonholes on most commercial shirts are vertical. Horizontal buttonholes are found only on very expensive shirts. (They cost more to make.) The more expensive the shirt, the better the details, right? It's your shirt.

I add an extra button to the tail—making seven—to keep the shirt from opening at the trousers.

To make buttonholes this way your sewing machine must have both a zigzag dial or lever to adjust the width of your stitches and a needle that moves to the left and right of the center position.

Mark the length of your buttonholes on your shirt-front. Use a pen or pencil so you have a narrow line to use as the center of the buttonhole.

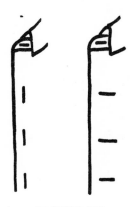

FIGURE 109

Swing your needle into the left position on the machine and set your zigzag width to one-half of the widest stitch width. For instance, my dial's widest setting is 4, so I set my machine at 2.

Set the length of your stitch to sew a satin stitch.

Bring the needle down by hand two or three times to make sure the needle is sewing to the left of your buttonhole line.

Zigzag the length of the buttonhole. Leave the needle in the material at the pencil line. Lift the presser foot, and pivot the shirt around halfway so the unsewn part of the buttonhole is to your left.

Lower the presser foot and bring the needle up out of the material.

Swing the needle to the center position. Turn your width dial to its widest setting (mine is now at 4).

Hold the shirt so it won't move, or set your machine to zero stitch length. Take five or six stitches across the end of the buttonhole. Bring the needle up out of the fabric.

Swing the needle back to the left, set the width to one-half width again (I'm at 2).

Do a couple of hand stitches with the needle again to be sure it doesn't sew too far to the right. Zigzag to the end of the pencil mark even with the first row of zigzag stitches.

Bring the needle up, position it in the center, turn to widest stitch, hold fabric, and take five or six stitches across the end of the buttonhole.

Vary the length and width of the zigzag stitches if you like until you think they look just like the ones on commercial shirts, but do it this way a couple of times to get the hang of it.

Now it's time to open the buttonholes.

Figure 110. Pierce the buttonhole with your seam ripper right by the keeper stitches on the side closest to the edge of the shirt.

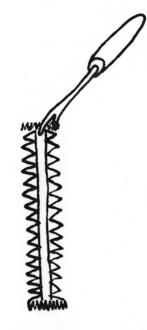

FIGURE 110

FIGURE 111

Figure 111. Remove the ripper and put a pin under the hole and outside both sides of the buttonhole stitches.

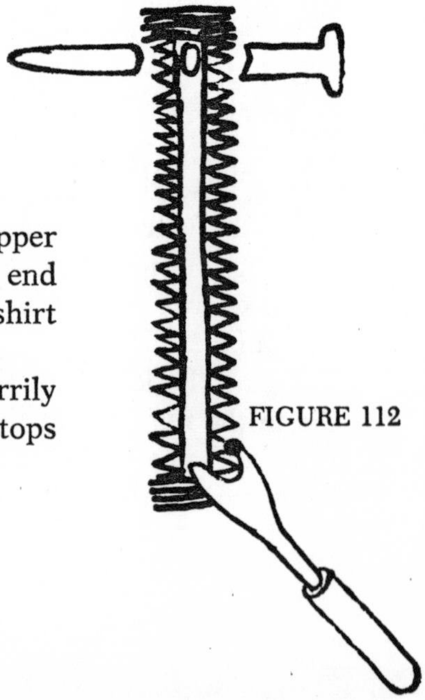

Figure 112. Insert the long point of the seam ripper at the other end of the hole. Make sure the balled end or small end of the seam ripper is up. Hold the shirt firmly behind the ripper and rip down to the pin.

If you put the balled end down, you will merrily rip over the pin and across the shirt. The pin stops the long point easily.

FIGURE 112

Figure 113. For mock French cuffs, make buttonholes on both sides of the cuff and sew the button to the end of the extra buttonhole. Open both buttonholes. Then the cuff can be buttoned or used with cufflinks.

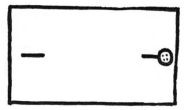

FIGURE 113

Buttons

Figure 114. For horizontal buttonholes, put the two sides of the shirt together, facings touching, and stick a pin into the end of the buttonhole. For vertical buttonholes, insert a pin in the center of the hole. Unbutton the pins and sew on the buttons.

Now, check that all loose threads are cut, and just look at that shirt. Isn't it a beauty?

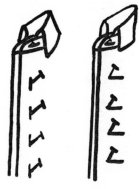

FIGURE 114

ADVENTURES IN ADVANCED SEWING

Everybody's welcome to these hints. But you should know how to sew and feel secure in that knowledge because these techniques require confidence—and guts—the first time around.

Notes on Knits

When constructing a knit shirt, follow the basic steps given for woven materials. The only difference will be the seams. Flat-fell seams don't work on knits, but the seams must be finished. Sew the regular seam plus a second seam outside, but close to, the first. Bind your edges with a zigzag or stretch stitch. If you want the flat-fell look, topstitch.

When you sew jersey or cotton knits, a regular stitch is not always recommended; these fabrics tend to stretch out of shape during the stitching. Sew your stretch stitch over a thread: Just lay the thread on the seam and sew over it. When you are finished, pull the seam into shape along the thread.

Figure 115. Sew narrow cotton twill tape into the shoulder seams on knits, so they won't pull out of shape. (You may also sew twill tape around the armholes if you like, but then the sleeves will pull out more readily since there's no give.)

FIGURE 115

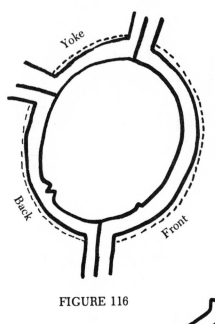

FIGURE 116

Quick Sleeve

The first step is to prepare the pattern.

Figure 116. Measure the armhole (front, yoke, and back). Do not measure the seam allowances; measure inside them from sewing line to sewing line.

Say you end up with 21 inches. (I have no idea what it will be for you, that is just a figure.)

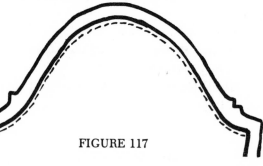

FIGURE 117

Figure 117. Measure around the sleeve. Call this 23¼ inches. This means you must take out 2 inches, since the sleeve has to be just ¼ inch larger than the armhole.

FIGURE 118

Figure 118. Fold the sleeve pattern in half. (Long or short, it makes no difference.) Mark the center fold at both ends. At the same time check to see that the sleeve seams match perfectly. If they do, leave them alone; if not, cut them to match. It makes for straighter seams and easier sewing.

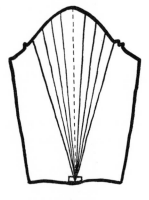

FIGURE 119

Figure 119. Open the pattern. We have to remove 2 inches—one on either side of the center. To keep the shape of the cap, we will do the removal in quarter-inches. Mark four straight lines, evenly spaced along the cap, to the center bottom mark on both sides of the sleeve. Put a piece of tape at the bottom mark.

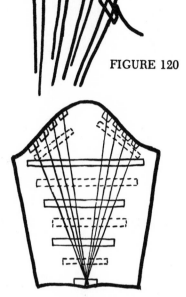

FIGURE 120

Figure 120. Cut the first line to the bottom mark, lap the pattern ¼ inch toward the side seam and tape. If you are careful, just the top is okay for now. Repeat all the way around. Measure again. The sleeve should be 21¼ inches.

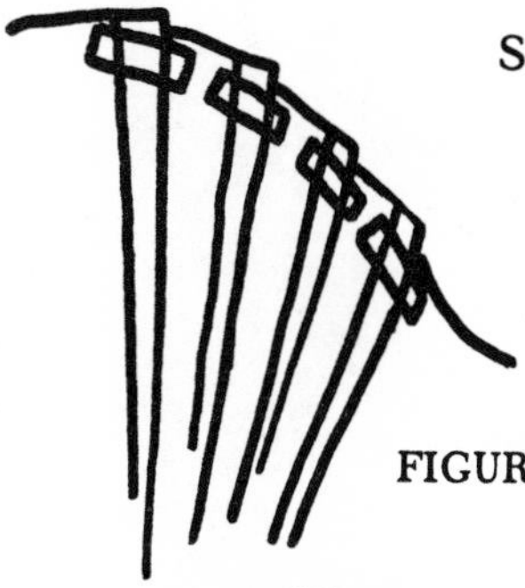

Figure 121. Lay the pattern flat and run tape across the cuts to keep it stable while you cut it out. (The dotted lines are tape on the underside.) Cut out the shirt and follow directions as instructed previously.

Here is where guts are required. With the sleeve down on the machine, lay the shirt on the sleeve. You will match the seam as you go. Just sew the pieces together keeping an even seam.

FIGURE 121

Figure 122. If you are having qualms the first time you try this, pin the shirt and sleeve together at the points shown in the illustration. (The sleeve is shown unpinned to make sure you get the pins on top at the shirt side of the seam. You sew with the sleeve down on your machine.) But you don't really need pins.

Sew and finish the sleeve in the regular manner.

Did you save enough time to make it worth your while?

You can sew all set-in sleeves this way, too. Bell sleeves, raglan, and tailored sleeves won't work though; just straight set-in sleeves.

One other trick here (not for men's sleeves, but for use on women's clothing): if you have a narrow sleeve in your pattern and you tend to pull the sleeve out at the armhole or your sleeves bind when you move, cut the sleeve on the bias. Some patterned fabrics won't allow this trick. But a biased sleeve is a joy forever!

Now, if you are happy with your pattern, it fits, it's easy to sew, it wears well, and you want to make more like it, cut the pattern out of nonwoven interfacing. The interfacing won't tear or stretch out of shape, and you will have a permanent pattern. Mark it with a ball-point pen and you are in business.

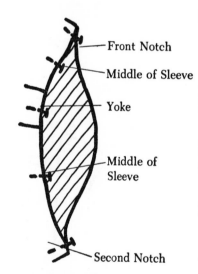

Front Notch
Middle of Sleeve
Yoke
Middle of Sleeve
Second Notch

FIGURE 122

Pinless Sewing

Match the sewing lines on your patterns. If they match perfectly, you can sew that seam without a pin. If they don't, mark them to match. Either cut away or add. If the sewing lines match and you cut carefully, most pinning is unnecessary.

The easiest way to explain this method is by using a two-piece skirt as an illustration. You have a skirt front and skirt back (the zipper is in the middle of the back to prevent complications). Match the *stitching lines* on each side so they are even. Don't match seam allowances. Cut ¼ inch from the seam allowance of the skirt front, all the way around. Now, with the back on the machine, match the skirt front, right-side down, to the upper waist corner. Sew down the seam to the hem. Turn the skirt so the lower hem corner is in the machine, the back is still down, and the skirt front is on top; sew up the seam to the waist.

When you match sewing lines and cut off that ¼ inch from the top piece, your seams will come out even without pinning.

Sewing for Boys

FIGURE 123

Figure 123. For a sport collar, take the shirtfront pattern and fold back the facing on the fold line. Trim away the facing at the neck edge until it is straight with the lower edge. Or fold the excess out of the way before cutting. When the collar is attached, all of the raw edges are hidden. Use the quick sleeve and the regular seam, eliminate topstitching across the yoke back, and eliminate shirt pockets if you like.

11 TROUSERS

Trousers aren't as difficult to sew as you may think. Study these directions first to see how they go together; it's simple and logical.

BEFORE WE BEGIN

For trousers we need a few things that aren't listed on the pattern back. Commercial belting may be available in your city. Call a few stores to see if they carry it, but don't waste a lot of time. I'll show you how to make some.

GETTING STARTED

Measure around the waist for his pattern size. Measure his favorite pair of pants from the inside of the crotch to the hem. That's his length.

You will need a pattern and a yard or so of sturdy-weight cotton or lining material, as you prefer, for pockets. Get large skirt hooks and eyes for the fly closing. Trouser zippers come in 11-inch lengths, but they don't come in many colors and the tabs are small; the 9-inchers come in lots of colors and aren't as sturdy, so make up your own mind about zippers.

Don't buy 7-inch zippers except for children's clothing. You will need ¼-inch twill tape to interface the belt loops. The next item may seem unusual, but it's necessary for belting: two yards of 3-inch drapery heading (if you can find a place that sells buckram, buy that instead). Buy the stiff kind of heading without perforations or pin pockets. It costs about twelve cents a yard. You will need three packages of 2-inch bias tape—either color coordinate, or use beige; a package of dark bias tape, the regular folded kind; and a package of 1-inch or 1½-inch horsehair braid (or, if you can find it, flexible belting. The stiff, cardboardy type won't work; it's too heavy).

TROUSERS SHOPPING LIST

Pattern
Trouser material
Yard of lining
Interfacing
1 package ¼-inch twill tape
1 package skirt closings (hook and eye)
2 buttons: 1 for pocket, 1 for fly
Commercial trouser belting if available, if not:
   2 yards of 3-inch drapery heading
3 packages of 2-inch bias tape
1 package of regular folded bias binding
1 package horsehair braid, *or*
1 yard flexible belting

CUTTING BASIC TROUSERS

Figure 124. Commercial patterns are usually large in the leg and waist. Measure your pattern, both front and back, from crotch to side. Now measure a pair of his favorite trousers. If there's a big difference, you'll have to pare the pattern down a little.

Back

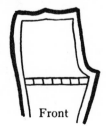
Front

FIGURE 124

Figure 125. You will have to take some from the back pattern piece. If the difference is one inch, remove one inch from your pattern along the back inside seam. Usually that's enough. But you can pare the sides a little. *Do not* change the front inner seam, you need all of that. Getting it close is good enough; extra waist can be taken up in the back seam.

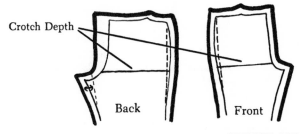

Crotch Depth

Back

Front

FIGURE 125

If his trousers normally ride up or pull down when he sits, you should alter the crotch on your pattern. Have him sit in a chair. Measure along his side over the hipbone from the chair seat to his waist. That is the crotch depth of his trousers.

You will find a line on both your front and back trouser pieces marked "crotch depth." Measure from the sewing line to the crotch line. That measurement and the measurement you made should be the same. If they are not, cut the pattern apart on the crotch-depth line and spread the pattern apart or overlay the necessary amount.

Figure 126. Find the middle of the front and the middle of the back. (Fold the pattern and you have it permanently.) Lay the pattern pieces so the middle line is on the straight grain of the fabric. Care must be taken at this point to ensure that the trouser legs will hang straight. The middle lines of the front and back pieces are where the crease of the trouser falls. Be sure to mark the center back seam sewing line with a piece of tailor's chalk for your adjusted waist measurement.

Cut the belt pieces at least 2½ inches longer than the pattern.

Cut just three fly pieces.

Follow the pattern if your pattern calls for back pockets, but make them 2 inches longer than the pattern calls for. If the pattern doesn't call for them, you can make your own very easily.

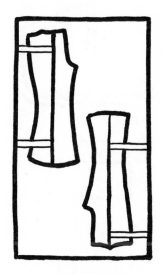

FIGURE 126

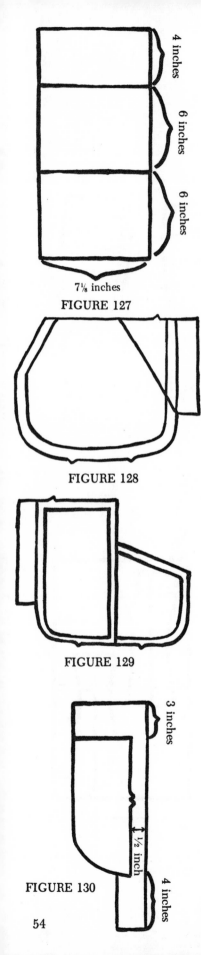

4 inches

6 inches

6 inches

7⅛ inches

FIGURE 127

FIGURE 128

FIGURE 129

3 inches

½ inch

4 inches

FIGURE 130

Figure 127. Most men find back pockets essential. Take your pocket lining material: cut two pieces twice the depth you want the pockets to be plus 4 inches—all together about 16 inches long by 7⅛ inches wide.

Figure 128. Now, take your pattern for the front pocket. On the side where the front facing is marked cut out an additional 1 inch of fabric from above the bottom of the facing mark up to the top seam. This piece covers the side seam neatly.

Front Yoke Pockets

Figure 129. Lay your pattern pieces down with seam allowances overlapping each other. Each seam allowance edge will match the sewing line of the other pattern piece. Place pattern pieces on the material and cut as one piece (but remember to cut two pockets). Also cut an extra inch from just below the facing to the top.

The Fly

Figure 130. You will need one other piece cut from the lining. Cut a right fly lining as follows: the tail is 4 inches long from the point where the fly starts curving in (it covers the front inside seam of the trouser); the straight side is ½ inch wider than your fly (it covers the inside seam of the fly); and the top is 3 inches longer (it makes a neat finish on the belt). Cut the notch.

Now bring out the pants fabric again. You will need four pieces, each 6¼ inches wide by 1¾ inches deep, for the back pocket facing and welt. You will also need two strips of interfacing the same size for the back pockets. Pattern pieces usually aren't quite big enough; measure them though—yours might be.

Belt Loops

The only other piece you'll need is for the belt loops: 1½ inches wide and 22 inches long, or as many pieces as you need for that length (that makes seven belt loops, 3 inches long plus 1 inch, just in case).

SEWING BASIC TROUSERS

Belting

Figure 131. We'll start with the belting. (If you were able to purchase belting, skip this section and start with the belt loops on page 56.) Start with the drapery heading. Measure in one inch and cut down its length.

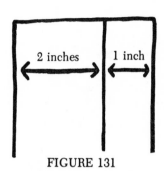

FIGURE 131

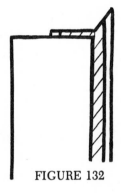

FIGURE 132

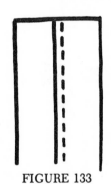

FIGURE 133

Figures 132 and 133. Fold one of your 2-inch bias tapes over the 2-inch piece of drapery heading. With your machine set on the longest stitch, sew down the length of the strip. Set the strip aside.

Figures 134 and 135. Now fold another 2-inch piece of bias tape over the one-inch strip of drapery heading and sew down its length with a long stitch. (Be sure you stitch through the heading.)

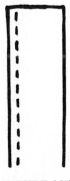

FIGURE 134   FIGURE 135   55

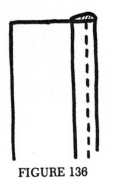

FIGURE 136

Figure 136. With the right side of the third 2-inch bias tape up, lay the regular folded bias binding on the tape. The open edge of the regular binding should be even with the edge of the wide bias tape. You will sew through one side of the 2-inch tape and both sides of the regular bias tape. Sew a ¼-inch seam along the two tapes.

Set your machine back to regular-sized stitches.

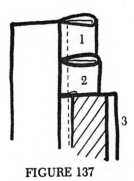

FIGURE 137

Figure 137. First lay the 2-inch strip of drapery heading down with the covered end facing your right (number 1 in the drawing).

The covered one-inch strip of heading comes next, its open edge even with the edge of the bias tape on the first piece (number 2).

The strips of bias (folded bias binding down) come next, the sewn edge even with the other two edges (number 3).

Sew them all together, keeping your stitching ¼ inch from the edge of the open bias strip and as straight and even as possible. Use the already-stitched seam as a guide.

Figure 138. Pull the wide bias binding strip (the third piece we put on) to the left to cover the 2-inch piece of heading. Press. Your belting will look like Figure 138. You will have enough belting for two or three pairs of trousers. Wash it, roll it up, use a clothespin to hold it, and set it aside until we get to the belt.

FIGURE 138

Making the Belt Loops

Figure 139. Belt loops, or carriers, need to be faced. Cut a length of twill tape 45 inches long. Double the tape to find the middle. Take the 22-inch-long piece of material. Fold the strip of material, right sides together, over the midpoint of the twill tape. Pin and sew a ¼-inch seam. Stitch only the material; don't get the tape in your seam.

FIGURE 139

Figure 140. Open the end of the seam by the twill tape and press. Just an inch or so. If you press the seam the entire length, when the tube is turned you have creases that are hard to remove. Stitch across the end several times so the tape is solidly attached. Now, getting the end of the belt loop piece to start through is sometimes difficult so cut the corners of the loop material, but *don't cut the tape.*

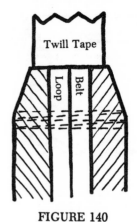

FIGURE 140

Figure 141. With one hand on the tape end, work the belt loop toward the tape. Pull the tape on the other end. Arrows show direction. After you get the end in, all you have to do is pull the tube down over the tape. Cut off the end with the stitching and the extra tape. Press so the seam is in the middle.

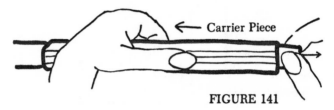

Carrier Piece

FIGURE 141

Back Welt Pocket

Although it doesn't make any difference which side of the material is right or wrong when you make your pockets, the illustrations show right sides as blank and wrong sides as lined to help you visualize your sewing.

I don't think pins are necessary for any of these straight seams, but if you wish to pin, by all means do so.

Figure 142. Take one of the 6½-inch strips you cut for the back pocket. With a piece of interfacing on the wrong side, zigzag down one long side of the strip. Remember to do both back pockets at the same time.

Figure 143. Place the strip on one end of the pocket —right side up, interfacing under, and the zigzag end toward the long piece of the pocket. Stitch across the top, making a ½-inch seam. Fold along the seam away from the zigzag edge (arrow shows direction) and press down.

FIGURE 142

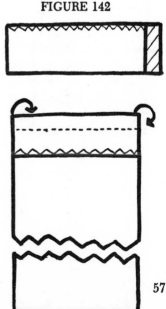

FIGURE 143

FIGURE 144

Figure 144. Turn the seam width in the same direction again (see arrow) using the bottom of the first seam as a turning guide. Turn the pocket over and sew across the welt as close to the bottom edge of the turn as possible. This is the back pocket welt.

Fold the pocket so that it is 5½ inches deep. The other 6¼-inch strip of pants material is centered inside the long end of the pocket, wrong side up, just below the stitching of the welt.

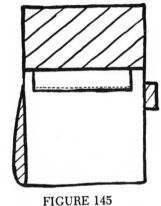

FIGURE 145

Figure 145 shows where the facing is positioned with the pocket closed.

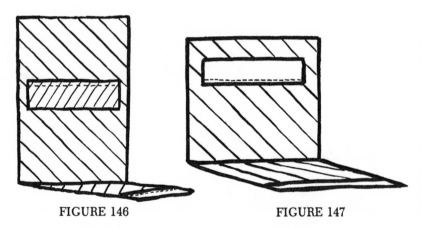

FIGURE 146   FIGURE 147

Figure 146 shows the facing centered after stitching a ¼-inch seam.

Figure 147 shows the facing pressed up. Topstitch ¼ inch from the bottom edge. We'll get the top edge when we put the pocket in the trousers.

Figure 148. Turn the pocket wrong side out on the bottom fold line. Pin. Position the top of the welt near the top of the facing.

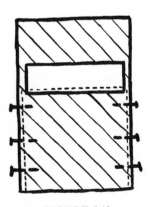

FIGURE 148

Figure 149. Turn the pocket over. Cut out the corners of the pocket by the welt from the outside edge up the welt sides. Just cut the welt side, not the facing side. Double dotted lines are the corners you cut out. The two straight lines down are stitching. Don't cut them. Stitch a ¼-inch seam on each side. (We are going to French-seam the pocket.) Turn right side out and press.

Figure 150. Stitch down both seams and along the bottom. Turn the edges of the top pocket at a slant toward the facing and welt. This piece goes next to the trouser back, so do it as it is shown even though it looks wrong. Stitch along the edges. Press. Put the pockets aside.

Take the back trouser pieces, mark the dart, and stitch it. If the pattern calls for a pocket, mark it and skip the next step. If not, . . . **Figure 151.** Measure 3 inches down from the top of the dart (the end of the dart will be below your mark). Mark a point 2⅝ inches from either side of the dart. Now make a dot ⅜ inch down from the first dots.

Figure 152. Make a slash between the dots to about ½ inch from them. Angle a cut to each dot.

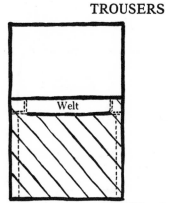

FIGURE 149

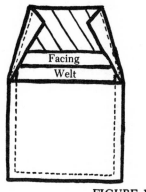

FIGURE 150

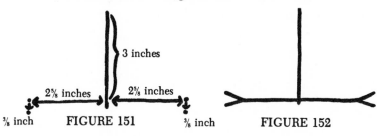

3 inches

2⅝ inches   2⅝ inches

⅜ inch   FIGURE 151   ⅜ inch   FIGURE 152

Figure 153. Open and press to the wrong side. Lay the trouser piece back, right side up, on a flat surface.

Figure 154. Pull the top of the pocket down and pin it out of the way. Pin the middle of the welt.

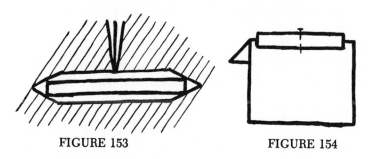

FIGURE 153   FIGURE 154

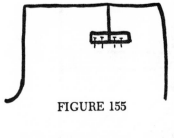

FIGURE 155

Figure 155. Slip the pocket under the trouser piece until the pin is even with the dart. The top of the welt will fit along the top creased edge of the slash and extend under on both sides. Carefully pin in that position, making sure the corners of the slash are tucked completely under the sides of the slash. The top slash will curve because of the dart. Do not let the welt go above the corners of the slash or he won't be able to get his hand in the pocket.

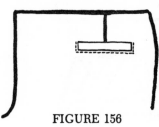

FIGURE 156

Figure 156. Stitch down one side as close to the edge as possible. Make sure you don't stitch the pocket top. At the corner leave the needle in the material, lift the presser foot, pivot the trouser piece, stitch along the long edge, pivot again, and stitch to the other corner. Remove from the machine. Press.

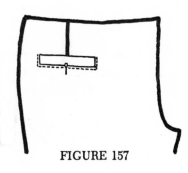

FIGURE 157

Figure 157. Make a buttonhole on the left side if you want a pocket that buttons.

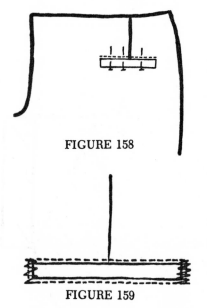

FIGURE 158

FIGURE 159

Figure 158. Pin the top of the slash to the top of the pocket. Smooth the pocket to avoid gathers and bumps. Holding the welt out of the way, stitch across the top from corner to corner. When the welt is in place it will cover these stitches. Remove pins and press.

Figure 159. Zigzag along the sides of the pocket using your satin stitch and the narrowest setting that will reach from the welt across the seam (about ⅛ inch). Sew through the pants back, the slash turnover, and the tail of the pocket. Make sure you cover the four corners or they will pull out. Pin the upper part of the pocket to the pants piece and set both trouser pieces aside.

Slash Side Pockets

Sewing the side pockets now may seem odd since the pattern calls for sewing the fly, but we would rather work with solid pieces, well attached. The fly is held together by the zipper, and it doesn't need the extra strain.

Figure 160. Open the pocket. Lay the large facing, right side down, on the open pocket ¼ inch inside the line marked on your pattern. Stitch ¼ inch in along the length.

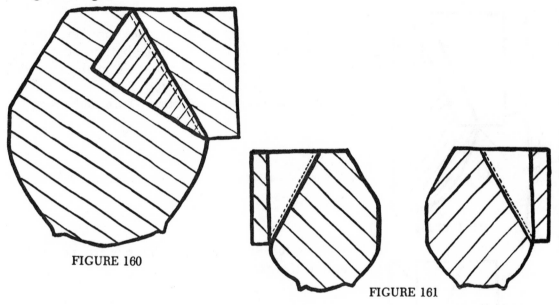

FIGURE 160

FIGURE 161

Figure 161. Press the facing toward the edge. Top-stitch along the facing from top to bottom. Make sure you do the other pocket in the opposite direction.

Figure 162. Cut a piece of interfacing to match the pocket facing. Lay the facing and interfacing right side down, with the interfacing on top. Again stitch ¼ inch inside the sewing line marked on your pattern. Press toward the edge.

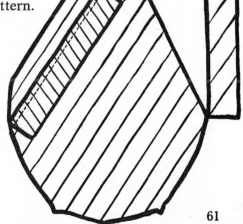

FIGURE 162

61

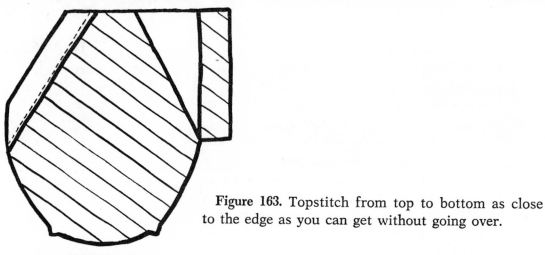

FIGURE 163

Figure 163. Topstitch from top to bottom as close to the edge as you can get without going over.

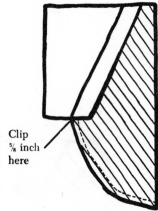

Clip
⅝ inch
here

FIGURE 164

Figure 164. With the right sides together, stitch a narrow seam (¼ inch) from the bottom of the extra piece we cut, around the pocket. Clip through both sides of the pocket at the top of the seam for full seam allowance; clip the curve. Turn and press.

Figure 165. Starting at the clip, sew around the bottom of the pocket.

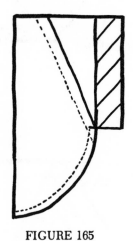

FIGURE 165

Figure 166. Pull the back part of the pocket down out of the way. Pin. Lay the front along the front trouser slash with the pocket facing and trouser right sides together. Pin. Stitch. Remove pins. Press seam toward the fly.

Pocket
Back

FIGURE 166

Figure 167. Turn the pocket under into place, and press with the pocket facing entirely covered by the trouser front. Keeping the back of the pocket out of the way, bring the pocket up as shown and stitch next to your first row of stitches. You are sewing both seam allowances to the pocket. This seam keeps the pocket along the slash from coming up and showing when the trousers are worn, or . . .

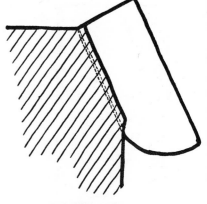

FIGURE 167

Figure 168. Topstitch ¼ inch from the edge of the pocket if you'd like the stitching to show. Pin pocket to trouser piece when you are done.

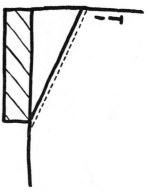

FIGURE 168

Yoke Side Pockets

Figure 169. Fit the yoke on the pocket piece. Turn under the hem, pin, and stitch. Cut a piece of interfacing to match the pocket facing. Turn under a ¼-inch hem on the strip used as pocket facing. Pin both the facing and interfacing to the pocket and stitch. Facing and yoke will overlap slightly. Remove pins and press.

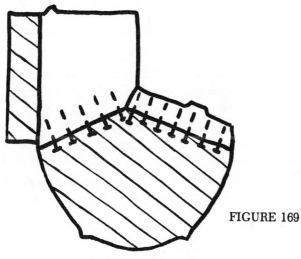

FIGURE 169

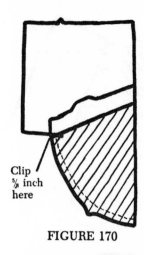

Clip
⅝ inch
here

FIGURE 170

Figure 170. Clip below the extra piece using the full seam allowance. Right sides together, stitch ¼ inch from the edge. Clip curved seam, turn, and press.

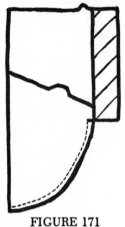

FIGURE 171

Figure 171. Stitch from the clip around the pocket.

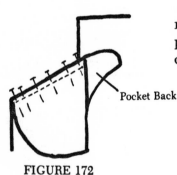

Pocket Back

FIGURE 172

Figure 172. Open pocket and lay the short piece, right side down, along the right side of the pants piece, matching notches. Pull the back of the pocket out of the way.

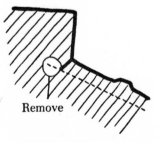

Remove

FIGURE 173

Figure 173. Stitch from the corner of the pocket angle on pants to the end of the facing. Remove pins. Clip the *pants* front very carefully from squarish corner to stitching. *Do not* clip the pocket—just the one layer of trouser material. Any stitching beyond the clip will have to be removed before you turn the pocket, or it won't turn smoothly. Press seam down, turn, and press.

Figure 174. Topstitch along the edge of the pocket. Bring the back of the pocket up. Turn raw edge of trouser front under and pin to back of pocket. Topstitch from top of trouser piece to the stitching across the pocket edge. Take a couple of extra stitches in the corner. Remove pins and press.

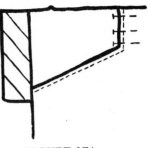

FIGURE 174

Figure 175. If you don't like topstitching, just fold the trouser piece toward the side, match to pocket edge, and stitch along the seam to the clip.

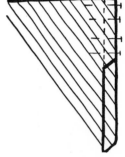

FIGURE 175

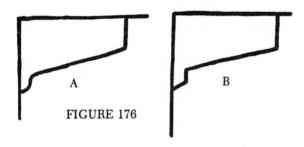

FIGURE 176

Figure 176. Pockets A and B can be made in the same fashion except the corners are cut into the facing and pocket pieces before the facing is sewn to the pocket.

FIGURE 177

Side Seams

Figure 177. Pin side seams with right sides together. On top match the pieces together with the extra pocket piece over the edge as shown. Pin the bottom of the pocket out of the way. Stitch and remove pins. Finish both side seam edges with a zigzag stitch.

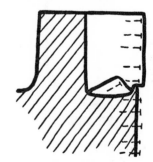

Figure 178. Turn a narrow hem in the extra pocket piece and turn it over the side seams; pin to both seam allowances. Stitch through both seams plus the turned piece of pocket to the end of the pocket piece. Remove pins and press seam toward the back seam.

FIGURE 178

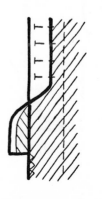

65

FIGURE 179

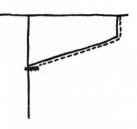

Figure 179. Turn pants right side out. Open. Using your satin stitch, zigzag (narrowly) across the end of the pocket for ⅜ inch. This relieves the strain from the pocket.

Left Fly

FIGURE 180

This is not as difficult as you may think. Cut a strip of interfacing the length of the fly and ½ inch narrower. It's not necessary to measure accurately. If your material is light, follow Figures 180 and 181; if you're using a knit or bulky material, follow Figure 182.

Figure 180. Put two left fly pieces together, wrong sides out. Stitch, letting the edge of the interfacing be barely caught in the stitches. Cut off the extra interfacing. Clip, turn, and press.

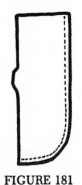

FIGURE 181

Figure 181. Topstitch about ¼ inch from the edge.

FIGURE 182

Figure 182. Sandwich the interfacing between the two fly pieces, which are placed wrong sides together, then zigzag along the edge. Make your stitches wide and not too long. Cut off the extra interfacing.

Figure 183. Pin the fly piece to the left front trouser, matching notches. Stitch to the small dot marked on your pants front. Remove the pins. Press the seam toward the fly.

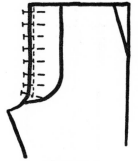

FIGURE 183

Figure 184. Clip the crotch seam to your row of stitches.

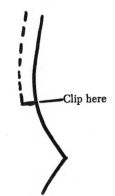

FIGURE 184

Figure 185. Turn the trouser piece over to the right side and pull the fly piece open. Lay the zipper face down along the seam. The bottom of the zipper should be ¼ inch above the small dot. The other end will extend over the top. About 1/16 inch of the fly should show to the right of the zipper.

Pin the right side of the zipper securely into position. Use one pin at the top of the zipper on the left side to keep the tape from moving (one at the bottom won't hurt either). Using a zipper foot, sew down the left side of the tape (the one closest to the edge of the fly). Remove pins. Open zipper.

Right Fly

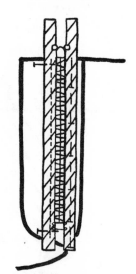

FIGURE 185

Figure 186. Take the right fly piece and the facing piece you cut. Sew them together along the curved edge. Clip and turn. *Do not* sew the notched edge.

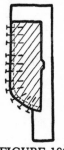

FIGURE 186

67

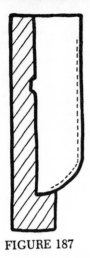

FIGURE 187

Figure 187. Sew a narrow seam beginning at the tail to one inch from the top.

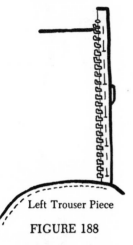

Left Trouser Piece

FIGURE 188

Figure 188. Match trouser fronts, using the fly notch as a guide so the zipper will be in the correct position when closed. Pin the zipper on the right side of the trouser front. Pull the left side of the trouser down out of the way. The edge of the tape should be even with the cut edge. Sew the zipper into place, removing pins as you sew.

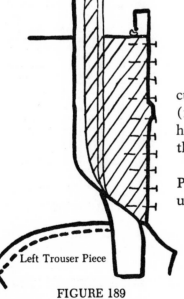

Left Trouser Piece

FIGURE 189

Figure 189. Open the right fly piece and lay the side cut from the pants material on top of the zipper (right side down). The lining is not stitched down here. Match notches, pin, and sew. Remove pins. Clip the trouser seam at the small dot.

Figure 190. Turn the whole shebang over and press. Pin the crotch seam below the fly to keep it neat until we get back to it.

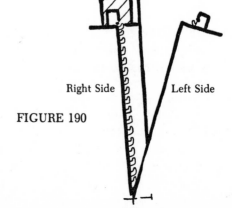

Right Side   Left Side

FIGURE 190

Belt

Take the belting you made or bought and cut two pieces: one the length of your belt pieces and one 2½ inches shorter.

Right Belt

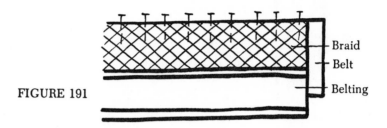

FIGURE 191

Braid
Belt
Belting

Figure 191. Using the longer piece of belting, with the belting facing you, extend the belt about ¼ inch to the right of the end of the belting. Measure a piece of horsehair-type belting from the edge of the zipper to the front pocket. Cut two. Put one aside. Then pin the belt, belting, and braid together as shown. Belt and belting should be with right sides together and the braid on top of the belting. Sew a ¼-inch seam down the length of the belt.

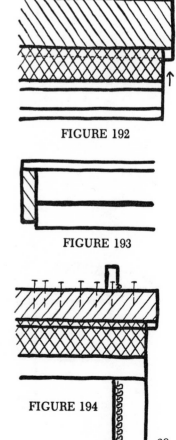

Figure 192. Press seam up toward the trouser belt piece. Arrow shows direction.

FIGURE 192

Figure 193. Using the top of the belting as a guide, press belt down so the belting is about ⅛ inch from the top.

FIGURE 193

Figure 194. Open again and pin belt to the right side of the pants. Extra length of belt will stick out from the edge of the fly. Do not sew the lining fly piece; hold it out of the way. Sew the seam. Sew between the teeth of the zipper, but take it easy or you'll break your needle. Remove pins and press belt up. Cut off any excess zipper. Just cut between the teeth; it won't hurt your scissors. You really can cut it, there are gaps between the teeth and you just cut the tape.

FIGURE 194

69

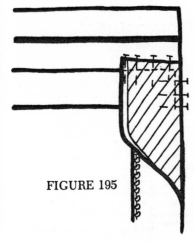

FIGURE 195

Right Fly Finish

Figure 195. Turn the fly lining to the right side of the fly. Pin it to the belt as shown. Pull a bit so the free end is higher than the fly edge. Pin it as close to the pressed fold of the belt as you can get. Fold a ½-inch hem on the free edge (fold it toward the fly on the outside). Pin along the fly edge using the ¼ inch or so of belt. Stitch as shown, just a touch above the crease; pivot at the edge and stitch down to the top of the belt. Remove the pins.

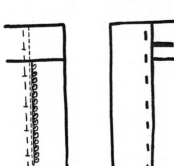

Front

Back

FIGURE 196

Figure 196. Turn the belting down and pull the fly facing over the corner. If you can, turn the corner without clipping; but if the turn is too bulky, by all means clip the corner.

Turn the ½ inch of the fly facing under and pin to the fly from the outside. Make sure all of the turn goes past the fly seam. Figure 196 shows both front and back with the pins on the underside. Use a zipper foot to topstitch from the top of the belt to the bottom of the zipper.

(Don't worry about that little tail; we'll use it in a while.) If the belt sticks out too far on the center back seam, cut it off. If it doesn't quite reach the end of the pants, it will be all right because the back seam is very generous.

Left Belt

Figure 197. Pin the belting and the belt with right sides together. The belt will extend 2½ inches from the left edge of the belting, with the belting side toward you. Sew a ¼-inch seam across the top. Remove the pins, press, and turn the belt as before.

FIGURE 197

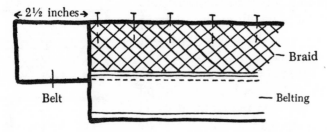

← 2½ inches →

Belt

— Braid

— Belting

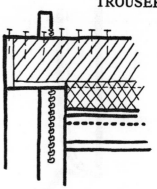

FIGURE 198

Figure 198. Open the fly. With the edge of the belting matched to the inside edge of the fly, pin belt to trousers (side seams should be pressed toward the back). Turn edge of belt to match fly edge. Sew. Remove pins and press seam toward top of belt. Cut the zipper as before.

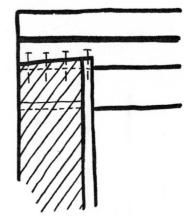

Figure 199. Turn the fly over the front. Pin the extra belt edge just by the creased top. Do not sew down the side of the fly. Stitch, remove pins.

FIGURE 199

Figure 200. Pull belting down into place and turn fly facing, without clipping corner if possible. Pin on outside of fly and topstitch to the end of the zipper, curving in to the seam. The material bunches a bit toward the end of the zipper, but persevere. Remove pins and press.

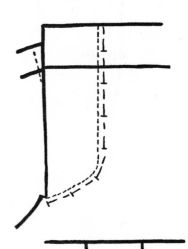

FIGURE 200

Figure 201. Now comes the test: Close the zipper. The belt tops should match. If they don't, go back and resew the top of the two sides of the belts until they match.

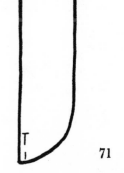

FIGURE 201

71

FIGURE 202

Figure 202. We cheat a bit here. Match the fly and pin, as shown in Figure 201. Turn the pants to the inside and sew about an inch of the crotch seam. Make sure the crotch is sewn past the end of the zipper. This is a trouble area because it takes a lot of strain. It's one of the first seams to split, so anchor it well.

FIGURE 203

Figure 203. Turn pants to the front. Using a satin stitch, sewing through both fly pieces from the outside, zigzag narrowly for ½ inch along the fly topstitching.

Figure 204. On the underside, match the left front and the right front fly pieces smoothly; zigzag with a satin stitch for ½ inch through both fly pieces.

FIGURE 204

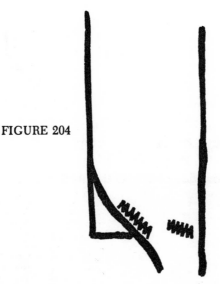

Inseams

Figure 205. Sew inseams with a straight seam. Match the trouser legs on the bottom. Are they both the same width? If not go back and sew the seam again. Finish individual edges with zigzag. Press open.

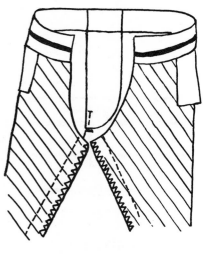

FIGURE 205

Back Seam

Figure 206. Match inseams, notches, and belt. Pin. Sew from the stitching already sewn by the fly and around the seam. Take a generous back seam. The belting should lie flat when turned; if it doesn't take an even more generous seam.

Fly Tail

Figure 207. Remember the tail on the fly facing? Turn a hem under on both sides. With the crotch seam open place two fingers on the outside of the trousers by the crotch seam. Pull the seam over the fingers making the crotch seam curve inward—just opposite its natural curve. Pin the tail to the inseam. Fold the end under. Be sure the crotch seam is pressed open or the tail will pull. Stitch through the facing and the seam allowance only on each side. Remove pins.

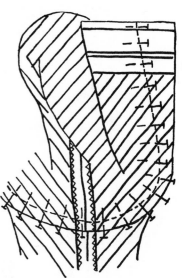

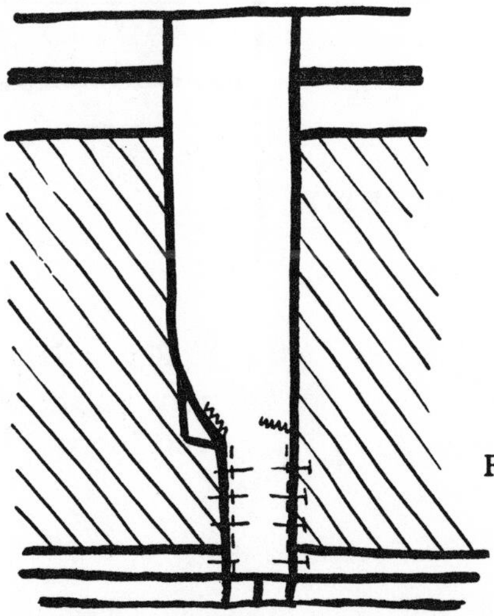

FIGURE 206

FIGURE 207

Attaching the Belt Loops

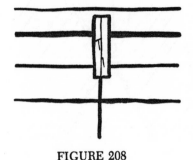

Cut your belt loop piece into seven 3-inch belt loops.

Figure 208. Pull the belting up. With the seamed side of the belt loop showing, pin each loop at the top of the belt ¼ inch below the crease in the belt. Pin the middle back loop first.

FIGURE 208

Figure 209. On the left side, place one loop just behind the front pocket and one between the two. Holding the belt loop by the front pocket, fold the belt toward the left.

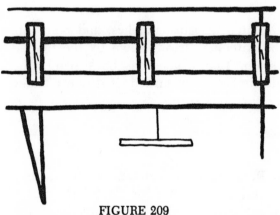

FIGURE 209

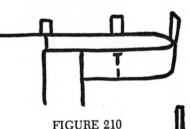

Figure 210. The front belt loop is positioned just in front of the middle belt loop as shown by the pin.

FIGURE 210

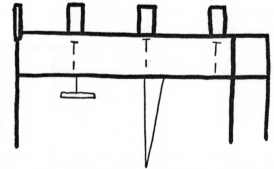

FIGURE 211

Figure 211. Fold the pants in half and put marking pins on the right side opposite the already-positioned belt loops. Pin belt loops into position.

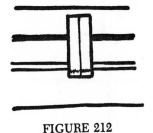

Figure 212. Do not sew the back belt loop yet. Sew the top of the other belt loops to the belt just below the crease. Use a narrow satin zigzag stitch. We'll sew the bottom and the back belt loop later.

FIGURE 212

Finishing the Belt

Figure 213. At the center back of the belt, turn the corners of the belting down toward the top of the belt and pin on the outside.

If you have a blind-stitch attachment use it for the next operation. Otherwise you can use your zigzag or do it by hand.

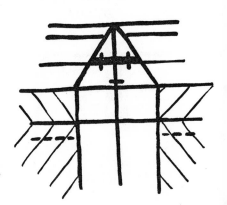

FIGURE 213

Figure 214. Turn the covering flap of the belting up and pin through the belting and the trouser belt.

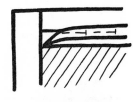

FIGURE 214

Figure 215. Turn the belt down toward the right side of the trousers. A quarter-inch of the belting flap will show above the trouser pocket. Blind-stitch the lower flap to the pockets all around. Sew just to the pockets, or . . .

To use your zigzag stitch: take three stitches, hit the zigzag button, zig into the pocket and zag back into the flap. Take three more stitches. Sew around the belt, catching just the pockets. Or slip stitch by hand around the belt, sewing just the pockets to the flap.

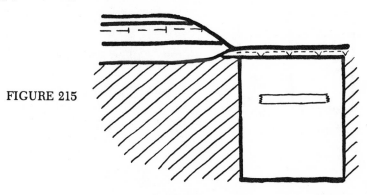

FIGURE 215

75

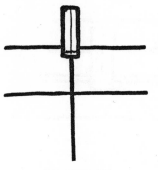

FIGURE 216

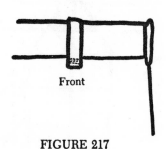

Front

FIGURE 217

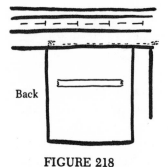

Back

FIGURE 218

Finishing the Belt Loops

Figure 216. Turn the belt up into place again, but don't unpin the belting top flap yet. The back belt loop is now attached with the satin zigzag, but sew through both the belt and the belting.

Figure 217. Turn the belt loops under (except for the back), and stitch across them with your regular stitch several times. You will sew through the pants, the pocket, and the lower flap of the belting. **Figure 217** and **Figure 218** show how both the inside and outside of the belt will look. Remove pins from belt flap.

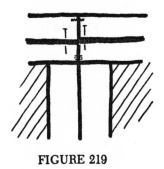

FIGURE 219

Figure 219. Stitch the back belt loop through all layers of fabric and belting. On the bottom, turn the back belt loop end up, and sew back and forth with the regular stitch. This keeps the ends of the belting up and out of the way. The belt loop also covers the seam. In case your belt pieces didn't meet exactly evenly, they won't show. Remove pins. Press.

Hems—Cuffed and Cuffless

Figure 220. Try on the trousers using a belt. Pin the hem just above the shoe in front. The back of the hem will be ½ inch longer.

½ inch

FIGURE 220

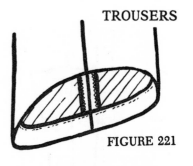

FIGURE 221

Figure 221. For a cuffless hem, just turn up and hem. Blind-stitch, zigzag, or sew by hand.

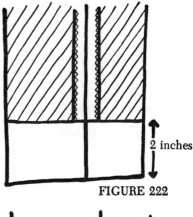

2 inches

FIGURE 222

Figure 222. For a one-inch cuff, turn under 2 inches. Hem, blind-stitch, or catch stitch by hand.

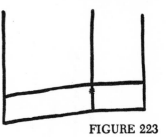

FIGURE 223

Figure 223. On the outside, turn cuff up and anchor at the seams.

Fly Closures

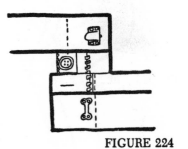

FIGURE 224

Figure 224. Attach the skirt closing hook and eye as shown. The hook is just above the zipper on the right side, and the eye just a touch toward the end of the belt on the left.

If you prefer the two-button closure, make one buttonhole in the fly and sew on the button. (For some reason known only to themselves, manufacturers call a closure with one button and one hook a "two-button closure." Expensive clothes usually have two-button closures.

FIGURE 225

Creases

Figure 225. To make a crease in the trousers, match the inseams and side seams. Pants should fall naturally into the crease. If they do, fine, press them. If not, try them on again.

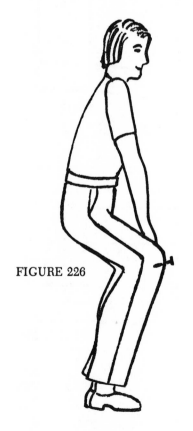

FIGURE 226

Figure 226. Ask the wearer to do a half knee bend and stop. Have two pins handy. Where the knees thrust out, the pants legs will fall naturally into a crease. Insert a pin right under the knee and press a crease at that point.

A permanent crease will only work on permanent-press fabrics: take a scrap of the pants material and make a mixture of one part water to one part white vinegar (cider vinegar will stain the material). Sponge the mixture on the scrap and press. If the fabric shows a bit of bleaching, use more water and less vinegar. Lay the pants on your ironing board, carefully arranged so the crease is exactly right. You only get one chance. When the trousers are arranged to your satisfaction, sponge them with the vinegar-and-water solution and press.

TROUSER VARIATIONS

Jeans-Style Pants

Jeans-type pants have yoked backs with an inset pocket. If you like this type of trouser but can't find a pattern, cut your pattern across the pocket line. Remember when you cut your material to add seam allowance on both pieces.

Figure 227. Mark the pocket placement on the bottom piece of the pants.

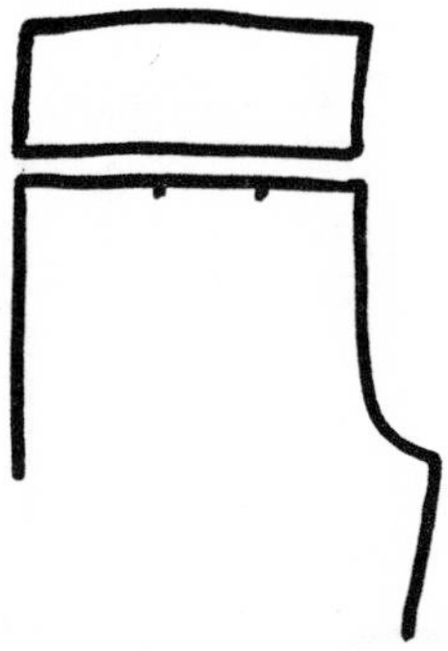

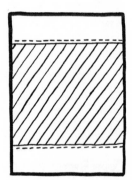

FIGURE 227

Figure 228. Face both ends of the pocket. Don't forget the interfacing.

FIGURE 228

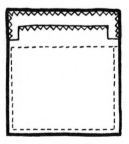

Figure 229. Pin pocket together, one side of the pocket about ½ inch longer than the other. Zigzag across the tops and French seam the sides. Cut out the corners of the short side as shown.

FIGURE 229

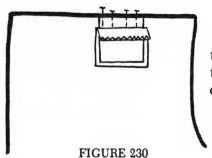

FIGURE 230

Figure 230. Lay the pocket on the pants piece with the wrong side of the short side to the right side of the pants. Pull the longer end of the pocket down out of the way. Pin.

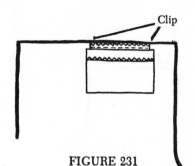

FIGURE 231

Figure 231. Sew a ½-inch seam across the pocket. Zigzag the pocket and pants seam edges together. Clip the pants piece to the seam as shown. Don't clip the pocket. Press.

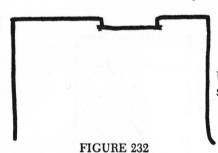

FIGURE 232

Figure 232. Turn pocket. Pull long piece down out of the way. Zigzag in the corners using a narrow satin stitch for ¼ inch.

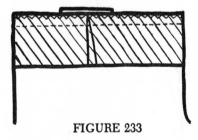

FIGURE 233

Figure 233. Sew the dart in the yoke; then fit the yoke to the bottom piece. Sew across the seam and the upper pocket. You will sew even with the top of the pocket, so pin the pocket on the lower piece out of the way if you think you might catch it in your seam. Finish the edges with a zigzag.

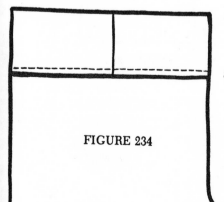

FIGURE 234

Figure 234. Pull the yoke up and press. Topstitch across the seam.

Yoke on a Boy's Jeans

Figure 235. Turn the seam allowance on the yoke, match notches, and lay yoke on top of pants bottom. Topstitch as shown.

Roll a small hem in the top of the pocket. Topstitch twice. Turn the seam allowance and apply pocket by topstitching twice.

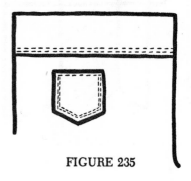

FIGURE 235

Boy's Belt

Turn a narrow hem in the unnotched edge of the belt and zigzag it down.

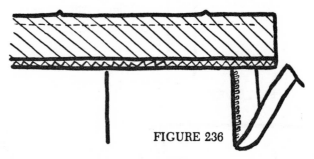

FIGURE 236

Figure 236. Cut a piece of flexible belting the length of the trouser top. Matching notches, with right sides together, lay the belt on the pants front. Pin and stitch.

Figure 237. Press seam up toward belt. Lay the belting so it is next to the stitch line. Stitch to belt across the top of the belting.

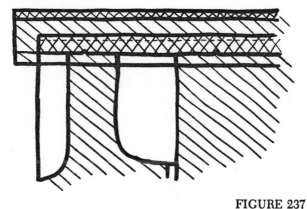

FIGURE 237

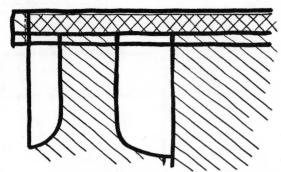

FIGURE 238

Figure 238. Fold the belt to the outside just a touch above the belting. Stitch the belt together on the ends, even with the top of the fly.

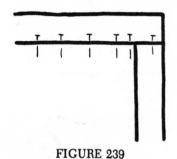

FIGURE 239

Figure 239. Turn the belt. Don't press yet. Pin the belt to the pants.

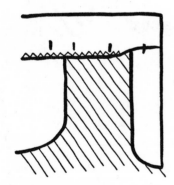

FIGURE 240

Figure 240. Turn the belt under by the fly. Everywhere else let it lie with the zigzag edge showing.

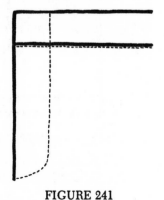

FIGURE 241

Figure 241. On the outside, stitch just below the seam of the turned belt. Remove pins. Press. The turn now covers the stitches. Topstitch the belt down to match the fly stitching.

Slip stitch the turnover by the fly if the row of stitching missed anything.

III LINED VEST

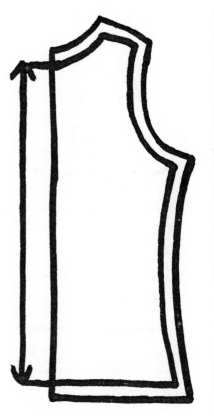

Vests may look complicated, but actually they are quite easy.

GETTING STARTED

Figure 242. Take a center back measurement from the big bone at the back of his neck to just below his belt. That is how long the vest should be. If you prefer, you may make the vest 2 inches longer than this to help prevent the shirt from sticking out between the trousers and the vest. Measure your pattern from sewing line to sewing line on the back piece and lengthen or shorten as necessary. Measure his waist and adjust side seams accordingly.

VEST SHOPPING LIST

Pattern-chest measurement
Vest material
Vest lining material
Interfacing
Buttons
Matching thread

FIGURE 242

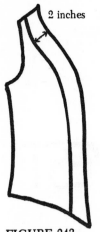

FIGURE 243

CUTTING THE VEST

Figure 243. Cut the pattern as directed in your pattern guide. If the vest has three pockets, cut three pieces of welt interfacing using the welt pattern. Cut two pieces of 2-inch-wide interfacing on the front pattern as shown. Mark the darts, pockets, and buttonholes.

SEWING THE VEST

Darts

Figure 244. Pin the darts. Be sure to stitch five stitches on the edge of the material before you start the dart. Sew along the dart line. Sew five stitches on the edge of the fold at the bottom. Remove pins and press. If you have a lot of curve in the piece when you press it and wish to make it lie flatter, clip the dart in the middle as shown. If that doesn't work, clip it a couple more times. (Don't forget to clip the darts on the lining when you get to them.)

FIGURE 244

Welts

Figure 245. Fit the interfacing to the welt.

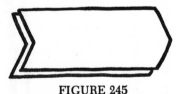

FIGURE 245

Figure 246. Right sides together, pin and stitch the short edges. Remove the pins.

FIGURE 246

Figure 247. Clip the corners and finger press the seams. Turn right side out.

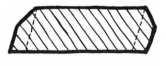

FIGURE 247

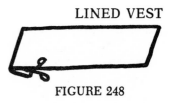

Figure 248. Press. Do all three welts (or two). Cut away that little corner sticking down from the turn.

FIGURE 248

Figure 249. The top pocket welt will be at an angle as shown. The lower pockets may be angled or they may be straight, so make sure your welts are also angled or straight.

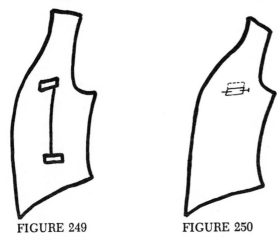

FIGURE 249 FIGURE 250

Figure 250. The welt goes on the outside of the front of the vest. Its seam line matches the bottom of the marking. Pin as shown to keep it from moving. The marking on the under pocket piece matches the marking on the vest.

Figure 251. If you have trouble matching the marks, stick pins in the four corners of the pocket piece. Then push them through the corners of the vest marking. The under pocket covers the welt.

FIGURE 251

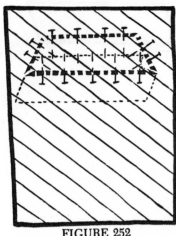

FIGURE 252

Figure 252. Pin and sew on the first short side. Keep as close to the edge of the welt as you can without actually running the needle through it. You can feel the welt under the pocket piece with your fingers. Large dots in Figure 252 show the stitching line. Small dots show position of welt under the pocket piece. Tuck the upper right corner of the welt down out of the stitching line as shown. Sew the bottom long seam the length of the welt. Next the other short side. Angle the two short sides up so that the last long seam is two or three stitches shorter than the bottom one. Remove pins.

FIGURE 253

Figure 253. Slash the pocket. Make the end triangles fairly large. Clip to your stitching line but don't cut the thread.

FIGURE 254

Figure 254. You can cut a thread or two of the material *under* the stitch as shown but be sure the stitching itself remains intact.

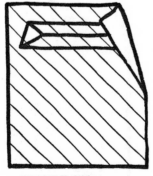

FIGURE 255

Figure 255. On the outside, press each edge of the pocket toward the slash, making four creases in the pocket piece.

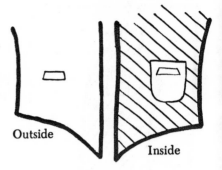

Outside

Inside

Figure 256. Pull the pocket through the slash. Roll the four slash edges to get a knife edge. Press the pocket piece. Then bring the welt up to cover the slash opening as shown.

FIGURE 256

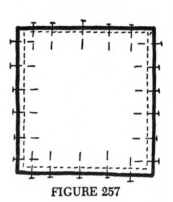

Figure 257. Pin the top pocket to the under pocket, matching notches. Holding the vest out of the way, stitch around the pocket. Remove pins.

FIGURE 257

Figure 258. Turn the vest to the right side. Fold the vest lengthwise toward the middle of the pocket, revealing the triangle. Stitch the triangle to both pieces of the pocket. Leaving the needle in the material, pivot the front. Fold the vest piece top to bottom to reveal the top of the slash.

FIGURE 258

Figure 259. Sew through the slash and both pocket pieces. Pivot at the corner, fold the vest lengthwise again, and sew through the other triangle.

FIGURE 259

FIGURE 260

Figure 260. Slip stitch the corners of the pocket to the vest if you wish. When finished, the back of the pocket will look like this. Finish all the pockets in this manner.

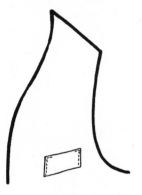

FIGURE 261

Figure 261. Pull the welt up so it covers the slash opening and pin into position as shown. If necessary, stretch both sides slightly to fit. Sew the welt to the vest through all layers. Take two stitches along the top, pivot, and sew down the sides as close to the edge as possible without going off the welt.

Seams

Sew the back and side seams of the vest. Press open. Put the vest aside. Sew the darts, and back and side seams of the lining. Press open. Cut ¼ inch from the seam allowance all the way around the lining.

Figure 262. With the interfacing in place, match seams and pin the lining to the vest, right sides together, as shown. Stitch along the front and bottom edges. The vest will bubble now but don't worry. Stitch the neck edge.

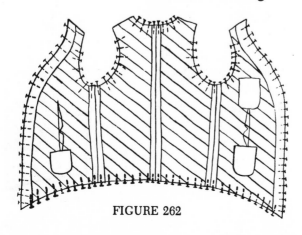

FIGURE 262

FIGURE 263

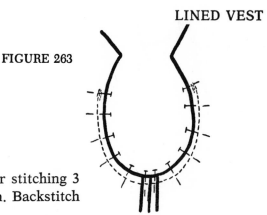

Figure 263. At each armhole, begin your stitching 3 inches from the shoulder seam as shown. Backstitch at each end of the seam.

FIGURE 264

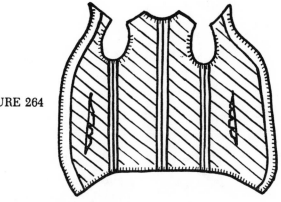

Figure 264. Remove the pins, and clip the curved seams and corners. Working through the openings, finger press the curved seams.

Turn vest by pulling the garment through one of the openings at the shoulder seam.

Figure 265. Roll the seams before you press. If any of them buckles, go back and clip that spot, working through one of the openings. Pin the side seams together if that helps you press more evenly. When the vest is pressed to your satisfaction, we'll finish it.

FIGURE 265

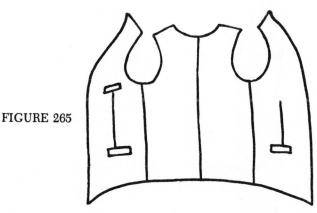

89

FIGURE 266

Figure 266. Match the shoulder seams of the vest from the inner neck to the shoulder. Stitch across. Remove pins.

FIGURE 267

Figure 267. Now you must do the same thing to the lining. (It's rather like building a ship in a bottle, but not really difficult.)

FIGURE 268

Figure 268. Turn under the remaining armhole seam allowance on the vest and lining and pin together. Working on the inside, slip stitch so the lining doesn't show. Remove pins and press. Topstitch if you like.

FIGURE 269

Figure 269. Work buttonholes by machine or by hand. Sew on the buttons.

IV TIE

Making ties is a snap. You'll wonder why you haven't tried it before. There aren't any particular measurements that will help you here.

TIE SHOPPING LIST

Pattern
Material
Lining—as lightweight as you can get
Woven tie interfacing
Nonwoven interfacing
Thread

CUTTING THE TIE

Cut away the lining on both upper and under tie pattern pieces, but allow yourself seam allowance on the tie ends. Make a lining piece for the big end of the tie by measuring up 4 inches on both sides. Figure 271 is how your lining piece will look.

Cut a lining pattern for the small end of the tie by measuring up ½ inch from the ends. Figure 277 shows how your lining pattern will look.

Figure 270. Now cut everything on the bias and you'll be okay. Cut the two pieces of tie, and the two lining pieces for the ends. Cut the two interfacing pieces from the soft woven interfacing and a strip of nonwoven interfacing the length of the wide tie piece and 1½ inches wide.

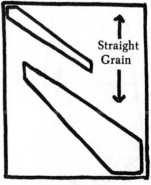

Straight Grain

FIGURE 270

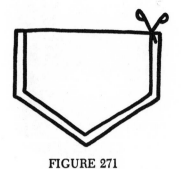

FIGURE 271

SEWING THE TIE

Figure 271. Cut ¼ inch from around the wide end of the tie lining.

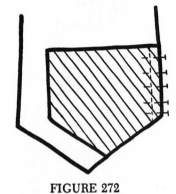

FIGURE 272

Figure 272. Right sides together, fit one side of the lining and tie together. Sew down the seam. Remove pins.

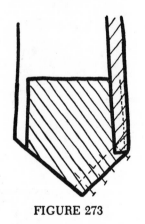

FIGURE 273

Figure 273. Turn first seam toward lining ¼ inch beyond the stitching. Pull lining to match tie edge and pin. Sew to the end of point. Remove pins.

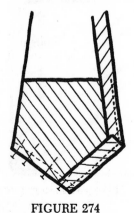

FIGURE 274

Figure 274. Turn seam toward lining—again ¼ inch beyond stitching. Pin. Sew. Remove pins.

Figure 275. Turn third seam as before toward lining. Pin. Sew. Remove pins.

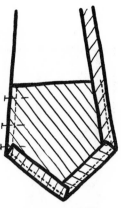

FIGURE 275

Figure 276. Turn last seam toward lining. Fold the tie to be sure the edges are even. Press. Turn lining right side out and press again.

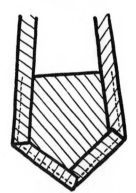

FIGURE 276

Figure 277. Cut ¼ inch from around the small end of the tie lining. Pin the lining on one side of the small end. Sew.

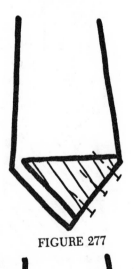

FIGURE 277

Figure 278. Pull lining over and sew the other edge. Lining will not come to the end of the tie.

FIGURE 278

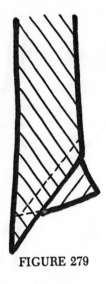

FIGURE 279

Figure 279. Fold the tie in half. Sew almost straight across the end of the tie as shown. Be sure to catch the point of the lining.

FIGURE 280

Figure 280. Fold the corner down along the stitching. Press into place.

FIGURE 281

Figure 281. Turn right side out and press.

TIE

FIGURE 282

Figure 282. Pin the two tie pieces together and sew the bias seam.

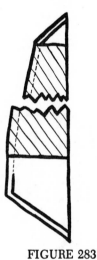

FIGURE 283

Figure 283. Fold the tie right sides together and stitch from the short end to just over the beginning of the finished sides on the wide end.

Figure 284. Pin the 1½-inch-wide strip of nonwoven interfacing from the bias seam to the beginning of the lining on the wide end. The middle of the interfacing will be along the seam. Sew using your longest stitch.

FIGURE 284

Figure 285. Sew bias interfacing strips together as in Figure 282. Pin interfacing to the seam—the middle of the interfacing on the seam. Sew down the length of the seam using your largest stitch. (Both sides of the tie are shown so you can see what you are doing.)

Turn right side out. Slip the end of the interfacing between the tie and the tie lining. Take a piece of cardboard and slip it into the wide end of the tie to press. Tack the top of the lining to the tie on the wide end.

That's it.

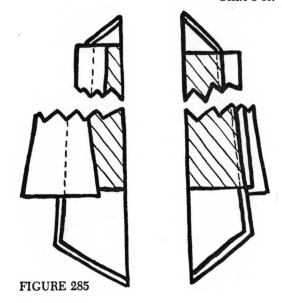

FIGURE 285

V SPORT JACKET

If tailoring a jacket scares you a bit, relax. Just take your time and all will go well.

BEFORE WE BEGIN

Before you buy your pattern, let us consider a few things. Basically, a jacket is a short coat. The styling of that coat is what makes it worth $65 and up. Pockets, set in or patch, patch with pleats, curved flaps, no flaps, stitched flaps, side vents, back vents, cuffs, cuffs with tabs, rounded points or square points on the lapels, wide or narrow lapels—all are just details. Don't look at them when you first consider a pattern.

Look for fit. Here is how a jacket should fit: the collar is close to the neck, one-half inch from the top of the shirt collar. Lapels lie flat, but the fold is never pressed in; it is achieved by the tailoring, with a roll by the top button. Sleeves hang straight from the shoulder with a slight forward curve to accommodate the curve of the arm, and they are never wide enough to be floppy. Sleeve length is just to the wrist, allowing one-half inch of shirt cuff to show. Slight fitting at the waist is achieved by a dart or a two-piece front.

The hem of the jacket should be even with the tips of the thumbs as his arms hang naturally at his sides. The back of the jacket should present a smooth line from the collar to the hem. When the arms are in motion, the collar and lapels are still flat, and no strain is apparent in the back of the jacket.

You can see that after you get a fit like this, the styling is easy.

GETTING STARTED

Before you go shopping, have him put on his favorite jacket. If it fits the way I described it, you're in business. If it doesn't, look at it closely. Where are the problem areas? Too short? Too long? Make a note of where it doesn't fit. Have him take the jacket off and get a tape measure.

Measure the back length, from the collar seam to the hem. If it is too short, add as many inches as you need; too long, subtract. That is your back seam length. Write it down. You know his chest measurement from the shirt. Put it down. (Check to see what size his jacket is; they should be the same.) Use the chest measurement for the correct pattern size. Hang the jacket on a hanger and measure the sleeve from the middle of the shoulder, right by the shoulder seam, straight down. The tape will fall just in front of the buttons. That is the sleeve measurement—unless you need to add or subtract. Write that with the other measurements.

While the jacket is hanging, look at its styling. You now know what you are looking for in a pattern. Buy a simple pattern that comes nearest in size to his chest and back-length measurements. But remember the more expensive the pattern the better the fit, which means you have less work to do.

There are two lining finishes for men's jackets. In a *fully lined* jacket, the inside is entirely covered with lining. Fully lined jackets are usually suit jackets. They are warmer than the half-lined ones and are quite handsome, because none of the inside seams show.

The other finish is *half-lining*. A half-lined jacket covers all of the inside jacket front and half of the jacket back. Half-lined jackets are usually sport coats and are lighter and cooler than the fully lined jackets. Most patterns are for half-lined jackets.

One thing before you buy material. Menswear calls for material especially made for men. Some fabrics may look lovely but are made for you—not him—and they won't wear as well. So buy from the men's section in the fabric store. Buy an extra ¼ yard for a plaid or napped fabric.

Buy the amount of hair canvas called for in the pattern plus an extra 1¼ yards. Be sure to buy the heavier canvas since you will need the extra bulk and body. Buy an extra ¼ yard of lining if you are making a half-lined jacket. If your pattern calls for a fully lined jacket, where both the back and front are lined, you will still need the extra lining. Buy the amount specified on the pattern back plus ¼ yard. If your pattern is a half-lined jacket and you would like to make a fully lined jacket, buy an extra ½ yard more lining than specified on the pattern back.

You may purchase shoulder pads, but it's easy to make them and you can be sure they will fit your garment. (Some of the hair canvas yardage is for shoulder pads.) For shoulder and chest padding buy Dacron batting—the kind that is used for making quilts. (It costs between one and four dollars, but I've gotten three jackets out of it so far and have barely touched the bulk of it.) You'll also need preshrunk twill tape, both ½- and ¼-inch widths; ½ yard of woven interfacing; some nonwoven interfacing, for pockets; buttons; and thread.

JACKET SHOPPING LIST

Pattern
Jacket material
Hair canvas (pattern amount plus 1¼ yards)
½ yard of lightweight woven interfacing
Lining (pattern amount plus ¼ yard for half-lined jacket)
Dacron batting
Nonwoven interfacing
1 package preshrunk ½-inch twill tape
1 package preshrunk ¼-inch twill tape
Buttons
Matching thread
Matching button twist

The total cost of materials will be about $25, based on $7 a yard jacket material.

ESSENTIAL PREPARATIONS

Preshrink dry-cleanable materials (or send them to the cleaners. If you do, be sure to send the hair canvas and interfacing too.) If you do it yourself, clip the selvages every 3 inches or so, or they'll pucker. Fold a wet sheet over the length of material and let it stand overnight on a flat surface. Wash the interfacing and the lining.

For washable fabrics, wash everything first.

Don't try to cheat and eliminate this step. In the end, shrinking your materials is a favor to yourself.

Before you get ready to cut, iron the pattern pieces. You can't afford the folds and wrinkles. Measure your back piece. Is it the same as the measurement you made earlier? (Remember that the pattern has an additional 1½ inches for hem.) Measure the top sleeve on the sewing line, from the center arrow straight down to the buttons. Subtract the hem allowance. If it's too long or short, adjust accordingly.

PADDING

First, let's make the padding. Jackets are padded not only on the shoulders but on the chest as well. The chest padding gives the jacket that beautiful straight look.

We will make two patterns, one for the shoulder pads and one for the chest padding. You need the jacket front and jacket back patterns. If the jacket front does not have the roll line on it, you will need the jacket facing pattern too. Get some newspaper and a marking pen.

Figure 286. Lay the jacket front on the newspaper; leave room for the jacket back above the shoulder seam side. The dotted lines show which part of the pattern we need. Fold the pattern straight down one inch in from the neck edge. Draw along this line until you are even with the sleeve notch. Trace on the sewing line around the pattern, starting one inch from

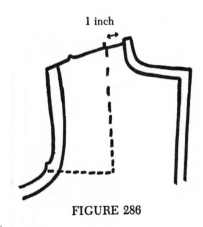

1 inch

FIGURE 286

the neck edge, along the shoulder line, and then—including the seam allowance—trace down to the sleeve notch. Remove the pattern and draw a line from the sleeve notch to the line down from the neck.

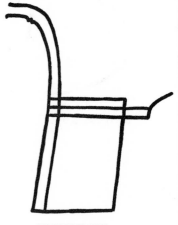

Figure 287. Lay the back pattern as shown over the pattern you just made with the shoulder seam sewing lines matching, and the shoulder seam allowances overlapping. Trace the armhole to the notches. Remove the pattern.

FIGURE 287

Figure 288. Draw a curved line from the neck to the end of the armhole line. Cut out the shoulder pad pattern.

Anytime you need a shoulder pad, make a pattern like this and you will have one that fits the garment perfectly.

The chest padding allows the wearer freedom of movement without wrinkling the front of the jacket.

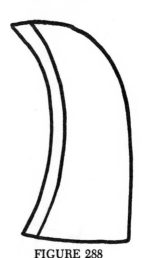

FIGURE 288

Figure 289. Check the facing and the front patterns. Lay them together and fold them both on the fold line. Put the facing pattern back in the envelope and mark the roll line on the jacket front. Lay the pattern on a piece of newspaper so that the top of the jacket is on the center of the paper. Trace from the roll line around the shoulder to the middle of the underarm, where you will find two little dots marked *underarm sleeve seam here*. Measure ⅝ inch in from the roll line at the center front. Measure 1¼ inches up from the end of the roll line. Make a dot where the two measurements come together. Draw a straight line from that mark to the beginning of your tracing at the shoulder.

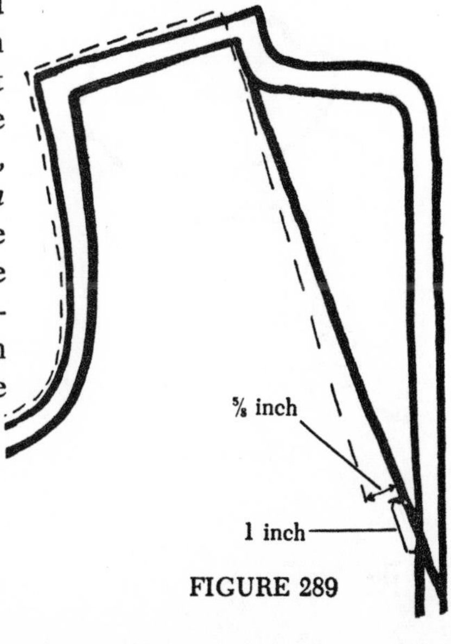

⅝ inch

1 inch

FIGURE 289

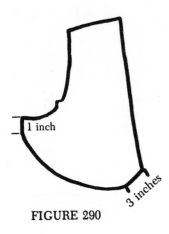

FIGURE 290

Figure 290. Draw a 3-inch straight line, parallel with the armhole, at the bottom of the new roll line. Then a straight line, parallel with the roll line, from the armhole line down about one inch. Draw a generous curve to match the lines together. Study Figure 290 and make your pattern as similar in appearance as you can.

Lay the extra 1¼ yards of hair canvas on your cutting board or table. Fiddle with the layout so you get four shoulder pad pieces and four chest pad pieces. Because the hair canvas is woven, keep the shoulder pads as close to the straight grain as possible. Since the chest pieces are padded and stitched, the grain isn't too important. If you do it right, you can lay the straight line of the chest padding on the fold line, which makes for easier assembly because you can place the Dacron padding right next to the fold. I think it's a bit easier than sandwiching the padding between two cut pieces. The hair canvas will stick to the padding because of all the little hair ends sticking out of the canvas, so using two pieces is not difficult. You also need two strips of hair canvas, each 2 inches wide and the length of the shoulder pad from the front sleeve notch to the rear sleeve notch. Measure along the seam allowance edge.

FIGURE 291

Figure 291. Lay a shoulder pad piece on one of the chest padding pieces, even with the notch. Trace around the shoulder pad on the chest piece. Mark two of the chest padding pieces in this manner. Be sure they are opposites.

Take the batting and cut four shoulder pads. Also cut two strips, each 1¼ inches wide and the length of the strips you cut previously.

Figure 292. Cut two pieces of batting, using the chest padding as a pattern. Cut along the outside, but cut out the marks you made of the shoulder pads. Dotted lines show where to cut.

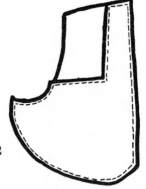

FIGURE 292

Figure 293. On two of the shoulder pad pieces, cut ¼ inch from the inside seam. Cut ¼ inch from the short straight seam.

FIGURE 293

Figure 294. Sew one uncut and one cut shoulder pad piece together along the inside seam, not the armhole seam. Pull the cut piece to match the uncut one so you have a bow in the shoulder pad. Use your longest stitch. Sew the other shoulder pad in the same manner but make it opposite the first.

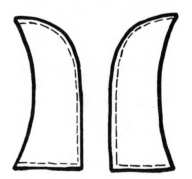

FIGURE 294

Figure 295. Stuff two of the Dacron batting pieces into each shoulder pad envelope. If you have a bump in the canvas, as shown, remove the stitches along the short seam, pull the bump out, pin, and resew so that when curved slightly both sides of the shoulder pad are smooth.

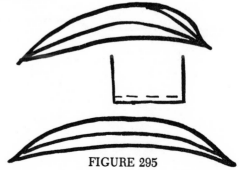

FIGURE 295

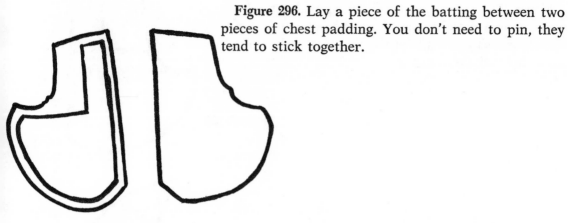

Figure 296. Lay a piece of the batting between two pieces of chest padding. You don't need to pin, they tend to stick together.

FIGURE 296

Start Here

Finish Here

FIGURE 297

Figure 297. With your longest stitch, sew down the long edge of the padding. Sew along the bottom until you are even with the mark for the shoulder pad. Zigzag up to the top, making your zigs to the line for the shoulder pad. Sew across the top and down. Sew around the bottom for an equal distance then zigzag up to the shoulder pad mark, across the top, and straight down again. Continue in this manner until the entire pad is sewn together. Do the other chest pad.

Figure 298. Lay the strip of batting on the strip of hair canvas. Turn over a generous seam—the strip should be about 1 to 1½ inches wide—the batting will not be completely covered, and stitch the length of the strip. Do both strips.

These pieces are for the sleeve cap. They push the sleeve out away from the arm and allow the sleeve to fall straight from the shoulder to the wrist.

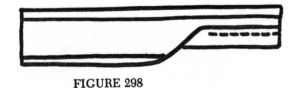

FIGURE 298

Figure 299. Cut a curve on the unsewn square corners.

FIGURE 299

Here is a good place to make your trial muslin jacket shell. You need the padding in the muslin shell to make sure the finished jacket will fit correctly. Turn to page 124; Figures 365 to 370 show how to attach the padding to the jacket. While you are working with the muslin, just pin the padding to your shell. When your pattern is adjusted to your satisfaction, remove the padding pieces and use them in the jacket. Your adjustments should not alter the basic shape of the padding, so don't worry about making the padding first.

Now you may put those pieces aside and cut out the jacket, the lining, and all the rest.

PATTERN LAYOUT

If you have a plaid or obvious pattern, you will have less trouble if you cut each piece separately. You will lay each piece on a single layer of material. When they are cut out, you will turn the pattern pieces over so the material side is up and cut each piece again.

If your material isn't plaid or doesn't have an obvious pattern, follow the pattern cutting instructions.

Open the material, place it right side up on a large cutting surface, and mark the middle line with pins or chalk. Lay out your pattern as called for on the pattern instruction sheet; remember the material is single so don't go past the middle line. Pin just the grain arrows. Measure from the top of the arrow to the selvage. Measure the bottom of the arrow to the selvage. If both measurements are the same you are on the straight grain.

To lengthen or shorten: pin the arrow on the top piece of the pattern just above the cut line. Cut the pattern and pull the bottom down or push it up. Measure the gap, or overlap. Say it's 2 inches, measure at both ends, making sure the grain arrow is in line, and pin. Now pin that piece to the material. Do this to the front, front facing, back, and sleeves on all of your materials—jacket, hair canvas, and lining. If you made your trial garment your pattern pieces won't need adjustment.

Make sure your back plaid matches the front plaid: when you lay out your pattern, lay each notch on each piece (front side notch to back side notch or front sleeve notch to back sleeve notch) at exactly the same point in the plaid. For instance, your plaid has three crosswise stripes and four up and down. Put the front notch in the first corner. Put the back notch in the same corner. The plaid will match crosswise and come as close as possible up and down, taking into account the contouring that goes into a jacket. Match the sleeve seams the same way.

The notches of the sleeve should match the pattern of the plaid by the notches in the armhole. Figure out how you want the collar to look and match it to the lapel of the facing piece.

Pin all the pieces but the pocket flaps and the undercollar.

This

CUTTING THE JACKET

Cut the undercollar in one piece. Remove the seam line and place the collar on a fold.

Cut the pocket flaps after everything else is cut out. Lay the flap pattern in place on the jacket front. When you know where the plaid is to fall for the flap, put the pattern on the material and cut out a matching flap.

You now have one-half of a jacket cut out.

Figure 300. Move the other half of the material onto your cutting surface. Lay out the pattern again, only

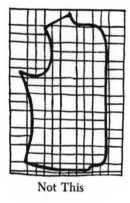

Not This

FIGURE 300

this time lay the pattern pieces face down (material side up). To match the plaid or stripe, arrange the piece you are placing so it disappears when the match is made, as shown in Figure 300. As soon as all the pieces match, cut them out. Again cut the collar and pocket flaps last.

Lining

Cut your lining as directed in the cutting instructions, lengthening or shortening pieces as you did for the main body of the jacket. Cut the rest of the lining fabric into 1½-inch-wide bias strips for a half-lined jacket—or as many as you think you may need to bind the back hem, the back hem edges, and two of the back side seam edges.

To cut a full lining when your pattern does not provide for it, take your back jacket piece, fold the lining material in half, and place the jacket pattern piece with the sewing line on the fold. Since the back seam is curved, the pattern will not touch all along the fold. Pin the pattern by the sewing line in the lower corner on the fold. At the neck, measure one inch from the fold, and pull the pattern so the neck sewing line is at that inch mark. Pin the neck there. Pin the rest of the pattern to the lining and cut it out. Mark that inch on the lining for the back pleat.

Interfacing

Figure 301. Cut the canvas interfacing from the remaining canvas. You need two pieces for the jacket front; one for the undercollar; two for the pocket flaps; one for the welt pocket—or another flap; one or two for the vents; two bias strips, each 2½ inches wide and the length of the sleeve hem; and enough 1½-inch bias strips to go around the hem of the jacket. Cut three bias strips, each ½ inch bigger around than the pocket slash mark on your pattern. Don't forget to lengthen or shorten the jacket front.

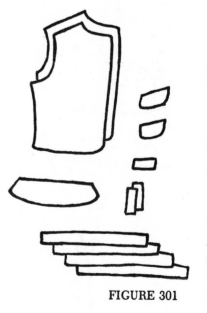

FIGURE 301

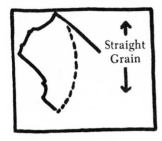

FIGURE 302

Figure 302. Fold the woven interfacing. Place the jacket back pattern on the interfacing so the grain arrow on the pattern is on the bias of the material. Cut around the back from the bottom of the armhole, across the shoulder, and around the neck. Remove the back pattern piece. Cut down from the armhole about 2 or 3 inches, and cut a generous curve up to the neck. Study Figure 302, and make your interfacing resemble it as closely as possible. If your pattern has a back interfacing piece, be sure to cut it on the bias. These interfacing pieces go on the jacket back to give the shoulders some body. You use woven interfacing and cut it on the bias so there is no bind or pull in the shoulders of the finished jacket.

If you took your time and cut the jacket correctly, you are bound to be pleased with the results. I can't emphasize strongly enough the importance of taking your time and doing it right when cutting out the jacket. I also can't emphasize strongly enough the importance of preshrinking the material and interfacing. Just imagine making a jacket, having it cleaned, and discovering that either the material or the interfacing has shrunk.

Marking

Marking the jacket is equally important, so again, take your time.

Figure 303. Mark the pockets on the front. If the front of the jacket has two pieces, be sure to mark both of them.

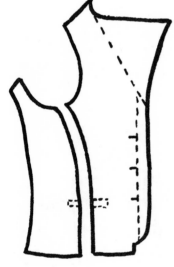

FIGURE 303

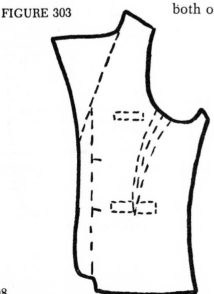

Figure 304. Tailor tack the darts: double your thread, take a small stitch, leaving a loop in the thread, take another small stitch, and cut the thread. When you remove the pattern, pull the two pieces of material apart and clip the threads between the layers, leaving thread on both pieces.

FIGURE 304

Mark the center front, the buttonholes, and the roll line. (Use tailor tacks, because tailor's chalk will rub off before you get to the sewing.) Mark the lining and the interfacing, too.

SEWING THE JACKET

These directions are for both fully lined and half-lined jackets. When the constructions are different, I'll say so.

Figure 305. The jacket dart is a contouring dart. It helps give the jacket a fitted appearance.

FIGURE 305

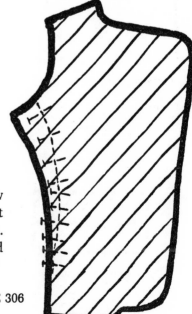

Figure 306. Match your tailor tacks and pin. Sew about five stitches as close to the edge as you can get just before you reach the first pin. Sew the dart. Backstitch on the armhole edge. Remove pins and tailor tacks.

FIGURE 306

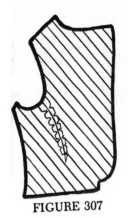

FIGURE 307

Figure 307. Cut the dart open as far as you can; but don't try to cut those five stitches. Clip the curved edges of the dart. Lay a damp cloth over the dart and press open, or . . .

FIGURE 308

Figure 308. If the jacket has a two-piece front, sew the two pieces together, easing the curve by careful pinning as you did for the two-piece shirtfront, Figures 56 and 57. Clip the curved seam edges and press. You can press your curves on the ham if you wish, but since the jacket is still basically flat, it is just as easy to press carefully on the ironing board.

Left Upper Pocket

If your top pocket is an inset pocket with a flap, turn to page 116 for instructions. Figures 331 and 333 show how to make the flap. Figures 336 to 347 show how to make the pocket and attach the flap.

You will need two pieces of jacket material for facing the pocket. Each should be 1 inch wider than the pocket slash; one should be 2 inches deep, the other 1½ inches deep.

Figure 309. Interface one-half of the welt. Pin. Stitch across on the underside close to the fold line.

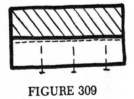

FIGURE 309

See Figures 246 to 248 for sewing the welt. Fold the welt so the right sides are together. Stitch the ends. Welt must match front pocket basting in length. Clip corners. Finger press side seams, turn, and press. Press this piece until you have knife-edges.

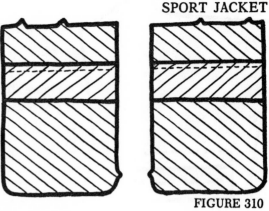

FIGURE 310

Figure 310. Sew the facings to the pocket pieces—the 2-inch facing to the under pocket. Match the top edges of the pocket and the facing. Then, leaving the bottom edge of the facing where it is, turn the entire facing down and sew across the top as shown, making a ¼-inch hem. Be sure matching facing is on the underpiece of the pocket.

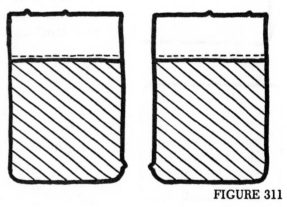

FIGURE 311

Figure 311. Press the facings up and topstitch along the edge.

Figure 312. Take the piece of interfacing ½ inch bigger than the pocket basting or slash. On the underside of the jacket, pin the piece of interfacing over the basting as shown in Figures 336 and 337. Turn the jacket piece to the right side and stitch around the slash just inside the basting.

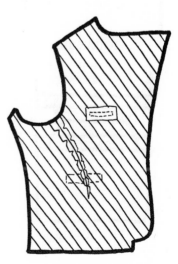

FIGURE 312

111

FIGURE 313

Figure 313. Lay the welt on the basting line, knife-edge toward the bottom of the jacket, with the bottom of the welt along the center of the slash mark. Pin.

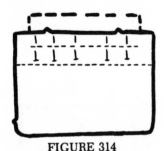

FIGURE 314

Figure 314. Lay the upper pocket on the welt, facing toward the jacket. Pin. Remove the pin holding the welt in place. Stitch just the long line of the pocket. If you'd like, turn the jacket over and stitch below the seam holding the interfacing in place. Be sure that your stitching does not go past either end of the welt.

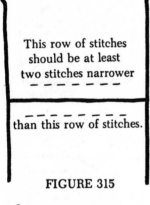

This row of stitches should be at least two stitches narrower

– – – – – –

than this row of stitches.

FIGURE 315

Figure 315. Lay the under pocket piece on the top of the pocket mark, facing down next to the jacket. The facing will cover half of the slash mark, meeting the welt and the other pocket piece in the middle. Pin. Stitch just the long seam again, making this seam two or three stitches narrower than the bottom seam at each end.

FIGURE 316

Figure 316. Slash the pocket open, but don't cut the lining pieces. Just pull them up out of the way.

Figure 317. Bring the upper pocket through the slash. Press the upper seam open. Turn the triangles and press away from the slash toward the edge of the interfacing. Stitch the length of the seam through the piece of interfacing, pulling the jacket front out of the way.

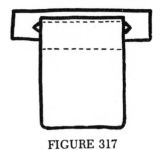

FIGURE 317

Figure 318. Turn the lower pocket. Press the welt into place. Be sure the welt covers the entire opening. Pin the welt to hold it in place.

FIGURE 318

Figure 319. Stitch the welt and the pocket seam to the interfacing on the underside. Hold the jacket front up out of the way.

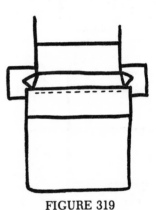

FIGURE 319

Figure 320. Stitch the pocket, still keeping the jacket front out of the way. Stitch through the interfacing, triangles, and both pocket pieces. Keep the material smooth.

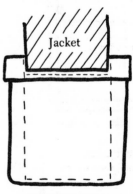

FIGURE 320

Figure 321. Pull one side of the welt over to cover the opening. Topstitch welt as shown—two stitches across the top and down the·side of the welt. Your stitching should be through the jacket front, the triangles, and both pocket pieces. Use small stitches and matching thread. Pull the other side over and stitch. Press.

FIGURE 321

FIGURE 322

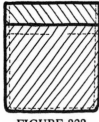

FIGURE 323

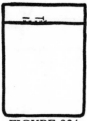

FIGURE 324

FIGURE 325

FIGURE 326

Patch Pocket

Figure 322. With right sides together, stitch the lining to the pocket along the straight edge, leaving an opening of 1½ inches in the center. Press the seam toward the pocket.

Figure 323. Still on the wrong side, match the edges, and pin. Sew around ¼ inch from the edge. (We need the rest of the seam allowance for the next step.) Finger press the seam, and clip. Use the opening to pull the pocket through. Press.

Figure 324. Turn the edge of the opening and, by hand, blind hem or slip stitch the top of the pocket to the lining.

Figure 325. Turn under the rest of the seam allowance. Press. Pin the edges down.

Figure 326. Position the pocket on the front of the jacket. Pin securely around the edge. With contrasting thread baste, as close as you can, around the *outside* of the pocket. Remove the pins and the pocket.

Figure 327. Make another outline of basting ⅛ inch inside the first row of basting stitches.

FIGURE 327

Figure 328. Pin the pocket with its edges along the inside basting. It will be bulgy, but don't worry. Now, using your biggest zigzag stitch, sew around the pocket. The zigzag is just to hold the pocket securely during the next step and will be removed. Remove pins.

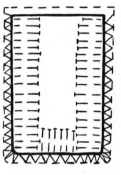

FIGURE 328

Figure 329. This is a bit difficult. Pull the pocket out of the way, stitch on the inside along the turned seam allowance. Cutaway view shows how it will look. This is easier said than done, I know, but try anyway.

After you've stitched around, remove the basting thread and zigzag stitches. Make a cardboard pattern the size of the pocket. Slip it into the pocket and press (it keeps the seam from making bumps in your pocket).

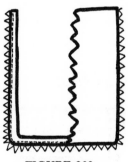

FIGURE 329

Figure 330. Topstitch ¼ inch in from the edge, taking two keeper stitches at the top, for a topstitched pocket.

FIGURE 330

115

Flap for Topstitched and Patch Pockets

The flap must be interfaced.

FIGURE 331

FIGURE 332

Figure 331. Cut ¼ inch from the seam allowance of the bottom piece of the flap.

Figure 332. With right sides together and interfacing on the bottom, match the ends of the flap. Gently pull the under flap to match the top as you sew. You are sewing this piece as you did the collar (Figures 39 to 42). When turned, the upper flap should be a bit larger than the under flap. Clip seams, finger press, and turn. Press again making sure that none of the under flap shows.

Finished flap for the inset pocket *must* be exactly the same width as the width of the upper edge of the pocket slash. If it is too wide the flap will pucker a bit, if it is too narrow you will leave a gap between the jacket and the flap. If you can't get it exactly right, make it a bit bigger, since you can always cut away but can never add to the flap after it's cut out.

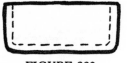

FIGURE 333

Figure 333. Optional: topstitch around the sewn edge ¼ inch from the edge.

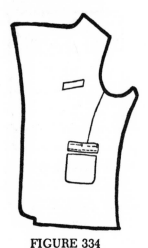

FIGURE 334

Attaching Flap

Figure 334. Lay flap, lining up, ¼ inch above the top of the pocket. Pin. Sew a ⅜-inch seam across the bottom straight edge, backstitching at the flap sides. Remove pins and press the flap down.

Figure 335. If any of the underneath edges of the flap stick out when the flap is turned down, cut those corners off. Topstitch ⅜ inch from the folded edge of the flap. The turned edge should be concealed when the flap is lifted.

FIGURE 335

Inset Pockets

Figure 336. Use chalk to mark the pocket opening on a piece of nonwoven interfacing.

FIGURE 336

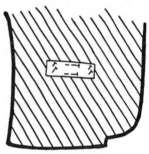

Figure 337. Put a pin through the jacket front at each corner of the pocket mark. Match the corners of the marks on the interfacing. Pin interfacing in place on the wrong side of the jacket front.

FIGURE 337

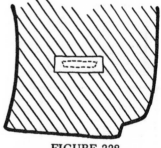

Figure 338. Stitch the interfacing in place, sewing just inside the chalked line. The top seam can be one or two stitches wider than the bottom seam. Slash open.

FIGURE 338

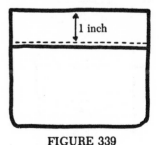

Figure 339. Cut a piece of jacket material 1½ inches wide. Turn under a ½-inch hem and sew the piece to the top of the pocket.

FIGURE 339

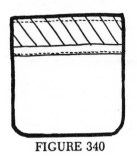

FIGURE 340

Figure 340. Do not sew the welt together. Place the welt piece at the top of the pocket with the welt and facing right sides together. Cut a piece of interfacing to match the welt. Sew the welt and interfacing to the pocket. Press the seam toward the bottom of the pocket.

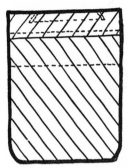

FIGURE 341

Figure 341. With the right side of the welt to the right side of the jacket, place the welt even with the long cut of the bottom of the slash. Double dotted lines show the slash under the pocket. Pin and sew the welt from one corner of the slash to the other. Press the pocket up as shown in Figure 383.

FIGURE 342

Figure 342. Turn the pocket to the inside. Fold the welt over the slash piece. The welt will cover one-half of the slash opening. Press the triangles away from the slash opening. Do this if you intend to topstitch your flap as shown in Figure 347. If you do not intend to topstitch the flap, bring the welt up to cover all of the slash opening.

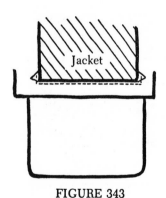

FIGURE 343

Figure 343. Pull the jacket front up out of the way. Seam as close as you can, down from the top of the triangle, across the bottom, and up through the other triangle. Although the triangles are shown in Figure 343, you will not see them when you sew this seam. They are between the interfacing on the jacket and the pocket piece. You will be sewing through the pocket, the welt, the slash, and the interfacing. Remove pins and press. Also, press the other half of the slash up.

FIGURE 344

Figure 344. Construct flaps as for the patch pocket, Figures 331 to 333. Make sure the flap material pattern matches the jacket material pattern. When you are satisfied, slip the open end of the flap under the pressed side of the slash and pin to the welt as shown.

Figure 345. Turn the jacket over to expose the interfacing and pin the flap to slash and interfacing. Sew across the top from one corner of the slash to the other. Again, triangles are shown, but they are under the interfacing. Remove pins and press.

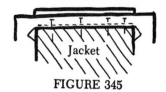

FIGURE 345

Figure 346. Pin lower pocket over the top pocket. Keeping the jacket front out of the way, stitch around the opening as close as possible and around pocket, keeping it as smooth as you can. Stitch through flap, slash, and interfacing on top, and triangles, welt, and interfacing on the sides—two pockets on the rest. The upper pocket will be longer than the lower pocket. Remove pins and press.

FIGURE 346

Figure 347. Turn the jacket over so the right side is up. Pull or pin the welt on the bottom side of the slash out of the way so you don't stitch the pocket shut. Sew through the bottom pocket and just to the edges of the flap.

Sew the dart and inset the pocket on the right side as in Figures 336 to 347.

FIGURE 347

Back

The methods for sewing the jacket back depend on whether it is fully lined or half-lined. In this section instructions are for the half-lined jacket. Separate directions for the fully lined jacket are given where the constructions are different. Also, look for the different constructions for the side vent and the back vent.

Figure 348. Sew the two back pieces together. Clip the notch from the seam allowance, or . . .

Figure 349. For a half-lined jacket sew the seam down past the top of the vent, but do not sew the vent pieces together. For a fully lined jacket sew the seam ⅝ inch past the top of the vent, pivot, and sew the top of the vent as shown. Remove the notch from the seam allowance.

If you are sewing a half-lined jacket, the center back and back side seam allowances are bound with

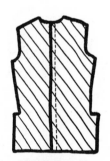

FIGURE 348

FIGURE 349

the bias strips you cut from the lining material. Follow the steps shown in Figures 350 and 351. If your jacket is fully lined, skip to Figure 352.

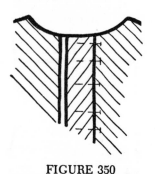

FIGURE 350

Figure 350. Get some of those bias strips you cut from the lining material. Lay the bias strip, right side down, matching its edge to the edge of the seam allowance—pinning first if you like. Sew down the length of the seam allowance using about ⅜-inch seam. If you have a back vent, sew down the right vent piece but not the left. On side vent jackets, sew the entire back seam allowance.

FIGURE 351

Figure 351. Turn the bias strips—folding for a hem is unnecessary, because the bias edges will not ravel. Stitch along the length of the seam allowance. Keep your stitching right beside the turn of the bias. This is called "stitch in the ditch" because, ideally, you put your row of stitches exactly between the edge of the seam allowance and the edge of the seam binding.

Now, press from the bound seam allowance toward the back seam. The bias will cover the stitching and the bound edge looks very neat.

Bind the other side of the back center seam and both side seams; on side vents, bind the vent edges the same way you did for the back seam allowance.

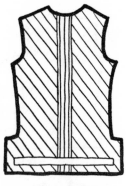

FIGURE 352

Figure 352. Lay one of the 1¼-inch bias interfacing strips ½ inch up from the bottom edge of the jacket. Use a catch stitch (Figure 353) to anchor the strip to the jacket.

Figure 353. Catch stitch: work left to right. Pick up no more than two threads of the jacket material. The needle goes in at the right under a thread, out on the left, over about ½ inch into the interfacing on the right, out on the left. Keep the thread behind the needle, and the catch stitch looks like this. Anchor the bottom interfacing all around the hem of the jacket in this manner.

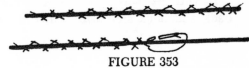

FIGURE 353

Back Vent

Figure 354. Place interfacing even with the back seam line on both vent pieces, shown in Figure 358, for both back and side vent jackets. Catch stitch as shown in Figure 353. For back vents, cut a piece of lining to match the left side of the vent, plus ½ inch in width. Open the vent, and on the outside pin the lining piece to the jacket vent, right sides together. Turn a ½-inch hem toward the edge of the vent in the top of the lining at the back seam.

Sew a ½-inch seam across the top and down the side. Clip the corner, remove the pins, and turn the lining over the vent piece. Finger press and roll the edges. Match the two vent pieces together and sew from the back seam to the edge of the vent. Clip the left vent from the corner to the stitching and hem. Slip stitch the vent edges to the back of the jacket. Leave the vent edges free from the back hem interfacing down to the hem.

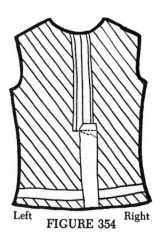

Left FIGURE 354 Right

Figure 355. For a belted back, interface the belt. Press the belt seam allowances under, and pin in place on the jacket back. Topstitch to the jacket back, being sure to sew both of the seams in the same direction. Sew over the back vent stitching. The left side of the jacket laps over the right as it faces you. Remove the pins and press.

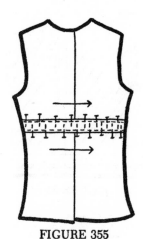

FIGURE 355

Figure 356. Sew bias interfacing pieces to the back, as shown, lapping the interfacing at the middle of the neck. Use a ¼-inch seam; do not sew inside the seam allowance.

FIGURE 356

Figure 357. With right sides together, sew the jacket fronts to the jacket back at the shoulder seam.

FIGURE 357

121

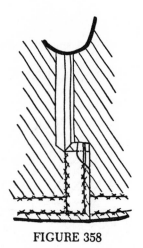

FIGURE 358

Side Seams and Side Vents

Figure 358. Right sides together, sew the side seams. On the side vents end the seam ⅝ inch below the top of the vents. Turn a ½-inch hem in the front vent seam allowance as shown. The bound edge of the other vent piece will be wider than the front vent piece. Pivot, and sew the top of the vents. On the side vent, clip the front piece to the stitching line and press the vents toward the back. Interface both vents on both sides, as shown.

The side seam on a jacket with a back vent continues to the hem.

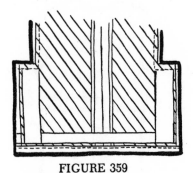

FIGURE 359

Figure 359. Bind back hem edge in the same manner as the back and side seams were done (Figures 350 and 351). Do not bind the hem of the fully lined jacket.

FIGURE 360

Figure 360. Turn the vents toward the back and stitch in place. Start at the seam and stitch, angling down slightly across the top of the vent.

Sleeves

Figure 361. Sew the sleeve seams. Sew the sleeve vent pieces together across the top of the vent. Clip the seam by the vent. Press both seams open. Tie a rolled-up magazine and use that to press the sleeve seams if you don't have a sleeve board.

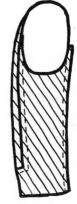

FIGURE 361

Figure 362. Place the sleeve interfacing one inch above the sleeve edge. Start at the upper sleeve; do not cover the upper sleeve vent, but do cover the lower sleeve vent. Pin around. Clip the excess. Catch stitch around.

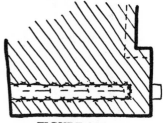

FIGURE 362

Figure 363. Right sides together, pin the sleeve into the jacket. Pin at the top, at the bottom, and at each notch on the sides.

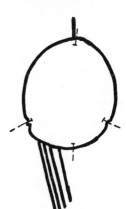

Figure 364. On the outside of the jacket, the back seam of the sleeve should fall about 4 inches below the shoulder seam. Measure your favorite jacket for the right amount. Pin the seam at that point.

FIGURE 363

Ease the sleeve into the armhole as you did for the shirt sleeve (Figures 89 to 92). It is exactly the same procedure, except you are working with a circle instead of a flat surface.

The underarm curves are bias, and they stretch; the sides and the cap, or top, of the sleeve have very little stretch.

Take your time and pin every pucker out of the sleeve or you will sew puckers into your sleeve in the finished garment.

The back seam of the sleeve should bisect the wearer's arm as he stands naturally. When he bends his arm, the seam should be right in the middle of the elbow. Baste the sleeves using button twist. We will have a fitting in just a bit. Set the jacket aside.

FIGURE 364

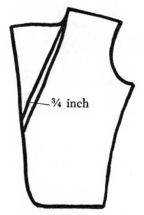

FIGURE 365

Interfacing and Padding

Figure 365. Mark the roll line on the jacket front interfacing. A pencil mark will do. Mark another line just outside that line at the top and up ¾ inch at the bottom.

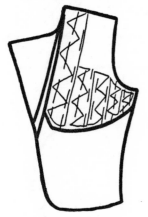

FIGURE 366

Figure 366. Position the chest padding along the inside line. Use running stitches to baste it to the interfacing everywhere but the opening for the shoulder pad. Cut away any piece of the padding that extends beyond the interfacing. Don't worry about cutting the padding stitches. It won't hurt anything.

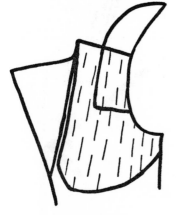

FIGURE 367

Figure 367. Insert the shoulder pad into the pocket between the two pieces of the chest padding. Figure 367 shows how the shoulder pad is positioned between the two pieces of the pad, right next to the stitches you made when you sewed the chest pad together. Now with running stitches baste them into place. Do not pull the basting thread tight enough to reduce the thickness of the shoulder pad.

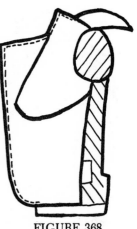

Figure 368. Fit the interfacing to the inside of the jacket. Baste along the stitching line around the front and across the shoulder. Make sure the interfacing lies flat on the jacket front. (Lay the jacket on a table; it helps you check to see that the interfacing is flat.)

FIGURE 368

Figure 369. Lay a piece of ½-inch twill tape along the roll line just to the end of the chest padding. Cut the tape ½ inch shorter than the length of the padding. Pin the tape at the top and machine stitch down the middle the length of the tape. Gently pull the tape to fit. The stitching will be on the underside of the lapel and won't show when you are finished, but be sure to use matching thread. Catch stitch the edges of the tape to the interfacing and padding. Do both lapels.

FIGURE 369

Figure 370. Turn the jacket right side out. Ball up your hand and hang the jacket over your fist. Your hand is pretending to be a shoulder. Place your fist so the edge of the hand will be at the end of the shoulder line (almost into the sleeve).

In this position the back of the shoulder pad falls naturally into place along the armhole as it will when the jacket is worn. Reach around to the inside back of the jacket with your other hand and mark the jacket back interfacing along the line of the shoulder pad.

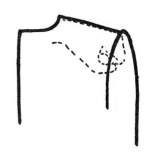

FIGURE 370

Laying the jacket on a flat surface or turning it inside out will position the shoulder pad either too high or too low along the armhole.

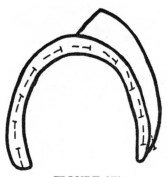

FIGURE 371

FIGURE 372

FIGURE 373

Figure 371. Open the jacket to the armhole. Pin the end of the shoulder pad to the mark you just made. Pin the front of the interfacing at the underarm.

Take one of the two long pieces of padded interfacing you made, Figures 298 and 299. Place the padding on the sleeve side of the sleeve seam. With the turned side down, the batting will face the open armhole; place the fold even with the seam allowance edge. Start pinning the end of the padding at the front sleeve notch. Keep the chest padding, shoulder pad, and sleeve padding even with the edge of the armhole seam allowance.

Keep the sleeve curved and pin the sleeve padding from the sleeve side of the armhole to the back notch. Pin through sleeve padding, sleeve seam, jacket interfacing, and jacket padding. On the back of the jacket pin the sleeve padding, seam allowance, and shoulder pad. Your row of pins should be along the row of basting stitches.

Figure 372. Try the jacket on. Turn the lapels and pin at the buttonhole marks. Is the jacket smooth everywhere? Remember your sleeves are just basted, so some wrinkles in them are allowable. The shoulders will be a bit straighter than you'd like, but after you sew the pads in they will slope more. The sleeves will come down a bit too, so keep that in mind. To even up shoulders, add padding to the low shoulder pad.

Figure 373. Pin the sleeve hem just at the wrist where the base of the thumb starts to swell out.

Back to sewing.

Figure 374. Remove the sleeve padding. Pin ¼-inch twill tape around the armhole along the stitching line. Stitch, holding the front interfacing and padding out of the way. Clip the seam at the notches and press the seam open along the top of the seam.

FIGURE 374

Figure 375. Repin the sleeve padding and hand stitch it into the sleeve along the open seam. Stitch the padding to the seam allowance.

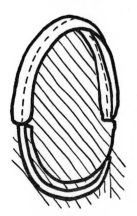

FIGURE 375

Figure 376. Hand stitch the chest padding to the shoulder seam. Stitch just the end of the shoulder pad to the interfacing with a couple of stitches.

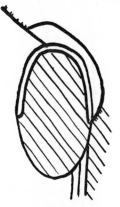

FIGURE 376

Figure 377. Lay the jacket on a smooth surface. Catch stitch, down the middle, the interfacing to the jacket front. Don't catch the pockets. Four or five inches is quite enough.

FIGURE 377

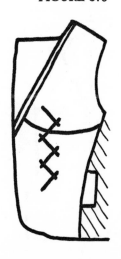

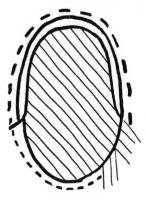

FIGURE 378

Figure 378. Using button twist and short stitches, baste the paddings to the sleeve allowance from the back notch to under the arm. Sew through the sleeve padding, seam allowance, shoulder pad, interfacing, and chest padding. You will have to sew one stitch at a time because of the thickness.

Close the jacket. Pin the front together on the baste marks for the buttons. Turn the lapel along the roll line. Hold your iron above the roll and steam the lapels until they lie flat. *Do not* touch the lapels or press a crease into them. Set the jacket aside on a flat surface until it dries.

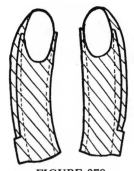

FIGURE 379

Lining for a Half-Lined Jacket

For a fully lined jacket turn to page 141. Where necessary you will be referred to steps in this section.

Figure 379. Sew the sleeve lining pieces together. Sew straight down on both sides ignoring the vent.

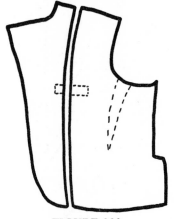

FIGURE 380

Figure 380. Mark the pocket on the facing. Mark the dart and the pocket on the lining.

Figure 381. Sew the facing to the lining. Press the seam allowance toward the armhole. Sew the dart. Cut the dart open and clip the curved edges. Press the dart open.

FIGURE 381

Figure 382. Pin a piece of interfacing to the wrong side of the lining covering the pocket slash marks as shown in Figures 336 to 338. Pin the pocket to the right side of the lining. The top of the pocket will be longer than the bottom. Stitch around the marks.

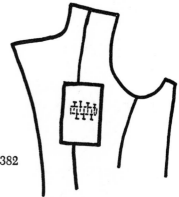

FIGURE 382

Figure 383. Slash through all thicknesses, making sure you have generous triangles on the ends. Pull the pocket up and press toward the slash, the triangles away from the center. The edges of the pocket tend to buckle because you aren't pressing against them, so watch them.

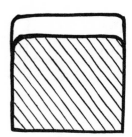

FIGURE 383

Figure 384. Bring the pocket to the inside. Leave the edges of the slash covered by the pocket. *Do not* press the slashed edges down. Do press the triangles out. Make sure they are pressed away from the slash. Pin the pocket in place with the edges smooth and even and meeting in the center of the slash on the right side.

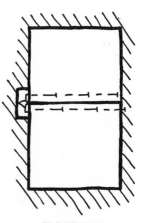

FIGURE 384

Figure 385. Topstitch around the pocket on the outside between the welt and the lining. Make your corners square. Remove pins and press.

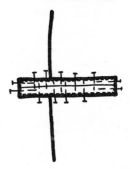

FIGURE 385

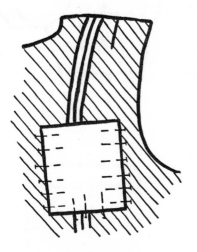

FIGURE 386

Figure 386. Turn lining over. Bring top of pocket down. Match edges with lower pocket. Keeping the jacket out of the way sew pocket to pocket being sure to catch triangles. Make another pocket in the other front lining.

FIGURE 387

Figure 387. Pin upper collar to facing. Turn the collar sides to the sewing line. Do not sew the collar seam allowances to the facing. Match notches. Stitch. Clip curved seams and press open.

Undercollar

Figure 388. Cut the seam allowance from the collar interfacing. Mark the roll line in pencil. Pin interfacing to undercollar and stitch along the roll line.

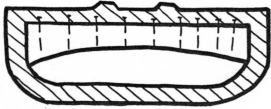

FIGURE 388

FIGURE 389

Figure 389. Turn the collar over and turn along roll line. Stitch down, across the bottom, back up to the roll line, across the top, and down to the bottom as shown. Continue in this manner across the bottom part of the collar. Keep the collar folded; this establishes the nice, sharp turn on the collar.

Figure 390. Stitch the same way on the top half of the undercollar. Or pad stitch collar as shown in Figure 397.

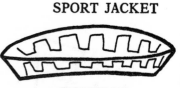

FIGURE 390

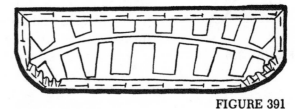

FIGURE 391

Figure 391. Turn the collar seam allowance over the interfacing and pin. Miter the corners as shown in **Figure 392, Figure 393,** and **Figure 394.**

FIGURE 392   FIGURE 393   FIGURE 394

Figure 395. Pin the collar, along the roll line, to your tailor's ham. Just stick the pins in as you would into a pincushion. Allow the roll line to fall naturally as it would around a neck.

Now hold your steam iron *over* the collar. (*Don't* touch it!) Steam the collar thoroughly. You want a sharp edge but not a crease. Don't worry about the rumples in the seam allowance; we'll get them later. You want the collar to hold its shape, so steam again. Set the collar and ham aside to dry.

FIGURE 395

Lapel

FIGURE 396

Figure 396. When your jacket is dry you can sew the lapel to the jacket. Sew as you did the undercollar, starting in the middle and working to the end, back to the middle and to the other end. Keep the lapel turned all the time, or . . .

If the stitching on the underside of the lapel bothers you, even though it won't show . . .

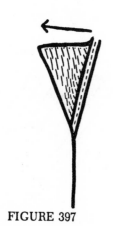

FIGURE 397

Figure 397. Pad stitch the lapel: picking up a thread of the jacket material through the interfacing, go down ½ inch or so, and pick up another thread of the jacket material through the interfacing. Starting at the roll line, work from top to bottom down the length of the lapel. The arrow shows the direction of your stitching. Make your rows of stitches progressively farther apart until you finish the lapel.

Sewing in the Lining

If you are making a fully lined jacket skip to page 141 (Figure 428).

Figure 398. Right sides together, match the lining to the jacket. If you did not sew on the stitching line when you sewed the collar to the facings, the collar and facings will not exactly match the front and neck edges of the jacket. Match the collar notches to the jacket; then pin the facings to the jacket lapels evenly. Allow any excess in the facings to extend over the jacket edge, or resew the collar to the facings until both the facings and the jacket fit. If you resew the collar, remove the first row of stitching so the seams will press flat.

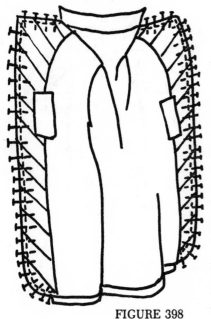

FIGURE 398

Starting at the middle of the collar, pin the bottom of the collar to the neck edge of the jacket, across the top of the lapels down the front edge of the jacket and around the curve (or across the bottom if your jacket has square fronts) to the end of the facing material. Do not pin any of the lining.

Do not sew the collar. Start stitching at the edge of the collar; stitch across the lapel, along the side, and around to the bottom of the jacket. Remove the pins.

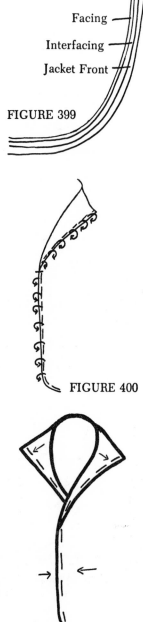

Facing
Interfacing
Jacket Front

Figure 399. Finger press the seams. Cut the facing seam allowance as close to the seam as you can. Cut the interfacing about half as much. (This is called layering and avoids the bulky seam look on the front when the jacket is pressed.) Now clip the curves.

FIGURE 399

Figure 400. I recommend basting on this step, because you are working with the roll of the collar and the flatter you get your lapels to lie the better. So, working on the outside and starting at the bottom of the jacket, roll the facing under the outside of the jacket. You don't wish any of the facing to show on the outside. When the facing is rolled out of sight, baste the jacket and facing together. Use small stitches and make your basting line ¼ inch from the edge of the jacket.

When you reach the bottom of the roll line, roll the jacket lapel under the facing. Arrows show the direction of the roll.

Baste the other side of the jacket the same way.

FIGURE 400

Figure 401. Press very carefully, keeping front edges and lapels going in the direction in which you basted them. Steam and steam and steam. When dry, they will retain their shape through washing or dry cleaning.

FIGURE 401

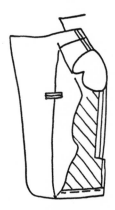

FIGURE 402

Figure 402. At the side vent, turn the jacket hem to the outside, even with the interfacing, matching the hem with the edge of the vent. Sew the hem to the vent as you do for the sleeve vent (Figure 410). Clip the corner and turn the rest of the jacket hem up to cover the interfacing strip. Press the hem turnover so it is just at the bottom edge of the interfacing. Do not turn the hem of a back vent jacket yet. Use a basting-type stitch to anchor the hem to the jacket, but be sure to catch only one or two threads of the jacket. Tack the front facing to the hem as shown. Tack the hem to the vent turn.

For a back vent jacket finish, position the sleeve and armhole seams as shown. Fold the side seam and baste into place. Do not turn the lining hem on the bottom of the back vent jacket.

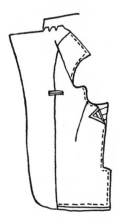

FIGURE 403

Figure 403. Match the lining to the jacket shoulder seam and baste the lining across the shoulder seam and around the armhole. Do not turn under a hem. Turn the seam allowance on the side, vent top (clip the corner of the vent if necessary), vent side, and jacket hem. Press the hem into the lining. Leave the corner by the armhole free for 3 inches along the armhole and down the side seam. Baste the lining to the jacket down the side, around the vent, and across the hem.

On the back vent jacket do the same, but ignore the directions for the vent and bottom hem.

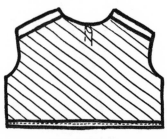

FIGURE 404

Figure 404. Make the pleat in the back lining. Sew a narrow hem in the bottom. Turn shoulder seam allowance down and press.

Figure 405. Baste the back lining to the armholes and side seams.

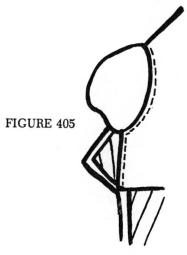

FIGURE 405

Figure 406. Cover the back lining with the free corner of the front lining. Baste.

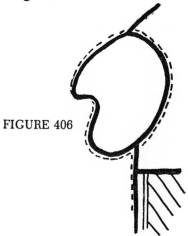

FIGURE 406

Figure 407. Hand sew the shoulder seams of the back lining over the front facing. Keep your stitches small and invisible.

FIGURE 407

FIGURE 408

Figure 408. Baste the lining at the neck until it fits. Machine stitch ¼ inch from the edge. Catch stitch across the pleat on the neck for an inch.

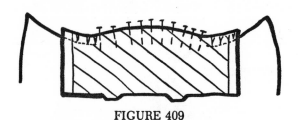

FIGURE 409

Figure 409. Bring the collar to the inside of the jacket—right side of the collar to the right side of the lining—and match the collar to the neck of the jacket. Pin, stitch, remove pins, and press the seam toward the top of the collar.

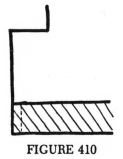

FIGURE 410

Figure 410. On the outside, turn up the jacket sleeve hem even with the pin you used to mark the length. Sew a ¼-inch seam along both vent sides. Finger press seam and turn. Now turn the sleeve inside out.

FIGURE 411

Figure 411. Press the vent to the inside along the fold line on the upper seam. Clip the hem edge until it lies flat, as indicated by the *V*'s in Figure 411. Pin around the bottom. Hand stitch the vent to the upper sleeve along the hem, and across the raw edge of the undersleeve.

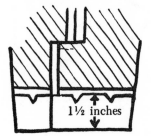

1½ inches

FIGURE 412

Figure 412. Measure the hem depth of the sleeve (say it is 1½ inches for demonstration purposes).

Figure 413. Now get the sleeve lining. Cut one inch from the lining hem. (The other ½ inch you measured on the sleeve hem is your seam allowance. You will cut off, roughly, two-thirds of the sleeve hem measurement from the sleeve lining hem.) Cut the vent off, too. It is not needed.

FIGURE 413

Figure 414. Pull the lining over the end of the sleeve, right sides together. Pin the edge of the sleeve lining to the edge of the sleeve hem. Sew around, leaving about 2 inches unsewn by the vent. Figure 414 shows how the edges look before they are pinned; the dotted lines show where your stitches go. Remove the pins. Pull the lining up over the sleeve.

FIGURE 414

Figure 415. Turn under the seam allowance by the vent and finish by hand. Turn the sleeves right side out.

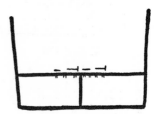

FIGURE 415

Figure 416. Working from the inside, pull sleeves inside out; pin the seam allowance of the sleeve over the seam allowances of the front and back lining. Dotted lines show sleeve position. Match your seams on the sleeves. You can stitch around it now or hang the jacket on a padded hanger overnight. I let it hang, because if the lining sags, you can correct it before the final stitching.

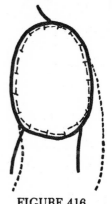

FIGURE 416

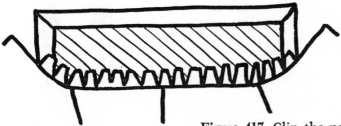

FIGURE 417

Figure 417. Clip the neck seam of the upper collar. Turn the seam allowance, mitering the corners as you did on the undercollar (Figures 392, 393, and 394). Baste and press.

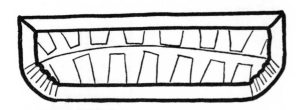

FIGURE 418

Figure 418. Take the undercollar and clip the gathers until the seam allowance lies flat.

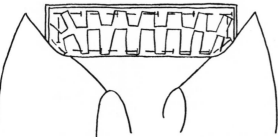

FIGURE 419

Figure 419. Lay the undercollar on the outside of the jacket along the collar. The upper collar will barely show on the top and sides. Match the undercollar to the seam line along the bottom. Hand stitch around the collar, keeping your stitches short and invisible. Remove the pins and turn the collar down. Now you can press it either around your ham or the short end of your ironing board. Don't press a crease into it though, just hold the iron above it and let the steam work for you.

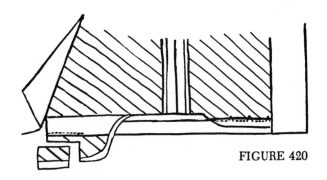

FIGURE 420

Figure 420. For the side vent jacket, turn the vents to the front. Sew across the bottom of the vent below the interfacing to the bound edge of the vent. Cut out the piece as shown on the left side of Figure 420. Finger press the seam and turn. Vent covers hem as shown on the right side. Do both vents; slip stitch the sides of the vent to the jacket; slip stitch the hem to the jacket.

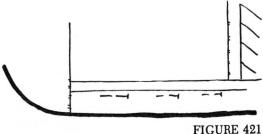

FIGURE 421

Figure 421. For the back vent, sew both vent sides across the bottom as shown in Figure 420. Pin the hem into position all around the jacket. Bring it up to cover the front linings. If the front facing and lining are sewn together so the hem will not slip under the facing, remove enough stitches from that seam to allow the hem to be covered by the facing. Slip stitch the facing to the hem. Slip stitch the hem to the jacket. Slip stitch the vent sides to the jacket.

Figure 422. When your lining has hung overnight, hand stitch around the sleeves, down the side seams, and across the front; stitch just the sleeves and side seam in a back vent jacket.

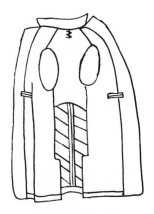

FIGURE 422

FIGURE 423

Figure 423. Now, if you like, topstitch around the jacket ¼ inch from the edge. Start at the bottom and sew around to where the collar and lapel are sewn together. Break your thread, move the collar into the machine. Sew the collar. Break your thread, move the lapel into the machine. Sew the other front. The gap between the two rows of stitches should be the width of your seam.

FIGURE 424

Buttons and Buttonholes

Figure 424. Punch a hole where the end of the buttonhole is to be placed. I use a leather punch because it cuts a very neat hole through all the layers of material. An eyelet punch will do the job, but be prepared to cut away some of the material around the punched hole. This hole leaves room for the thread holding the button so the button sits flat on the jacket and keeps the buttonhole from bunching up. Cut a slit the length of the button. Using button twist, stitch by hand around the buttonhole. Make small stitches and sew as close to the slit as you can.

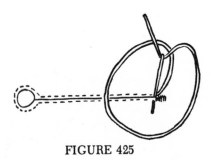

FIGURE 425

Figure 425. Circle the thread counterclockwise around the buttonhole. Take a narrow stitch (but cover the row of stitches you made) and pull the thread through. The needle will go through the loop made when you circled the buttonhole (this stitch is called tailor's buttonhole stitch). Continue in this manner all around, making your stitches as close together as you can.

FIGURE 426

Figure 426. On the end of the buttonhole take two long stitches, the width of both sides of the buttonhole. Work several stitches along the long stitches.

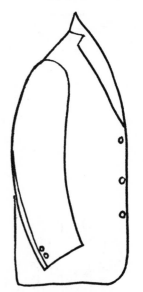

Figure 427. Sew two, or three, buttons on the sleeves and two or three on the front, as you wish.

And there you have a jacket!

Take it to the cleaners and ask them to press it. Just a press. You won't believe what a difference it makes.

FIGURE 427

Fully Lined Jacket

Construct jacket as before, omitting bound side and back seams. Bind hem (Figures 350 and 351). Sew facing and jacket front lining together with darts and pockets (Figures 380 to 387). Complete undercollar as shown in Figures 388 to 395. Pin pleat in back lining (Figure 404). For a two-piece back lining, sew back, then pin pleat (Figure 404). Some patterns have an extension instead of a full pleat; if this is the case with your pattern, follow your stitching lines, then pin the pleat toward the left back.

Sew front and back together. Cut out the vent on the left side of the lining for the back vent and on the back of the lining for the side vents.

Now, there are two ways to sew in the lining. Method one:

Figure 428. Match front facing to jacket and pin. Upper collar will be between jacket and lining. Sew around, leaving bottom free. Clip curved edges. Layer seams as in the half-lined jacket (Figure 399). Turn and press. See Figure 398 for pinning jacket; see Figure 399 before turning lining; see Figure 400 to finish the edge of the jacket.

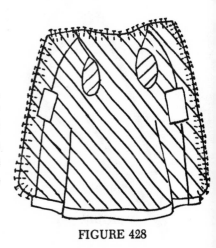

FIGURE 428

FIGURE 429

Figure 429. Turn hem up and blind-stitch along hem. Hand sew lining to vent edges. Attach undercollar (Figures 418 and 419).

Finish sleeves as for the half-lined jacket (Figure 413).

Method two:

Make the lining as before and sew the sleeves into it.

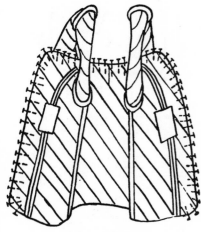

FIGURE 430

Figure 430. Sew the sleeves together as explained in the half-lined jacket (Figure 414).

Pin the lining to the jacket (Figure 430 and Figures 398 to 400). You will have to break the thread and start again by the sleeves when you sew around the jacket. Turn sleeves right side out. Pull lining over and press.

Finish bottom hem as for back vent hem, Figure 421. Attach undercollar (Figures 418 and 419). And you have a jacket.

DETAILS, DETAILS, DETAILS

As I said before, details are what make or break a jacket. Now that you have a jacket that fits, you can change the details as you wish to keep it in fashion.

Lapels

Recently, lapels have gone wide. Look at your pattern picture. Are the lapels wide enough to suit you?

Figure 431. Just add as much to the lapel as you wish. Lay the pattern on a piece of newspaper and widen the lapel. Do the whole pattern piece over, or just the lapel. Pin the extra on the pattern. Don't forget to make the facing to match and to buy extra material.

Round the corners or narrow the lapel. Whateve you do, do it to both pattern pieces

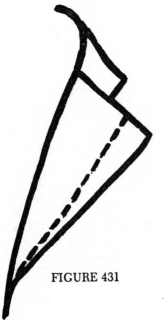

FIGURE 431

Pockets

Figure 432. Pockets are many and varied. One of the most popular is the pleated pocket. Slit the patch pocket pattern in half and add 4 inches in the middle for a 1-inch pleat. Keep the lining the same and the pocket won't sag. Pleat to the inside. Dotted lines show where the pleat falls on the underside of the pocket.

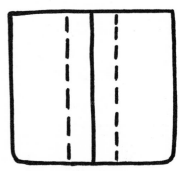

FIGURE 432

Figure 433. Pleat to the outside: dotted lines show where the pleat falls on the underside of the pocket.

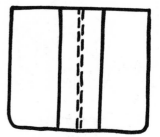

FIGURE 433

Figure 434. Use the same pocket you put in the lining on a lightweight summer jacket. Do this on all three pockets. This pocket may or may not have a flap.

FIGURE 434

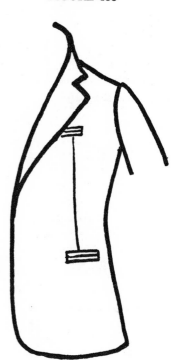

FIGURE 435

Figure 435. Flaps on pockets with buttons: simply add a buttonhole and a button. If you like, that point on the flap can be moved. Here it is close to the side. Figure 347 shows it in the middle.

FIGURE 436

Figure 436. The bias banded pocket: cut the patch pocket on the bias with a straight band across the top. The lining must be on the straight grain to prevent sag.

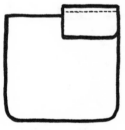

FIGURE 437

Figure 437. Make the top left-hand pocket a patch pocket with or without a flap. Put the same pocket on the upper right side, too.

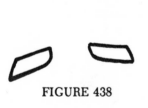

FIGURE 438

Figure 438. Cut the flaps and welt out of contrasting material. If you are working in a light, patterned knit, choose one of the dark colors and cut the flaps out of plain material.

FIGURE 439

Figure 439. Use a contrasting color of thread to stitch for a decorative touch on lapels and patch pockets.

How about four buttons on the sleeves?

A monogram or crest on the upper pocket?

When you walk through the stores look at the jackets, those for sale and those on men shoppers. Anytime you see a detail you like, remember it; when you get home sketch it on a piece of paper. Incorporate it in your next jacket. Use your imagination and keep sewing. But most of all, have fun!

BIBLIOGRAPHY

General Sewing and Alterations

Hutton, Jessie, and Cunningham, Gladys. *Singer Sewing Book*. Revised edition. New York: The Singer Company, 1972.

McCall's Sewing Book. Revised edition. New York: Random House, 1968.

Musheno, Elizabeth, J., ed. *Vogue Sewing Book*. Revised edition. New York: Vogue Patterns, 1973.

Perry, Patricia, ed. *Ready Set Sew*. New York: Butterick Fashion Marketing Company, 1971.

Pattern Making and Alterations

Moore, Dorothy. *Pattern Drafting and Dressmaking*. New York: Golden Press, 1971.

Nordquist, Barbara K. *The Complete Guide to Pattern Making*. New York: Drake, 1974.